MACLEAN
OF DUART

MACLEAN OF DUART

The Biography of 'Chips' Maclean

Brian Hoey

Country Life Books

PHOTOGRAPHIC ACKNOWLEDGEMENTS

The photographs in this book are from the private collection of Lord Maclean with the exception of the following:
Colour British Rail 120; The Illustrated London News Picture Library 119; Jarrold & Sons Ltd 26 top, 26 bottom; Michael Plomer/Country Life Books 25, 118 top; Syndication International 117 top.
Black and white David L. Bankes 66 top, 66 bottom; Srdja Djukanovic 149 bottom; Jarrold & Son Ltd 62 top, 152; The Scots Guards 67 top; John Scott 145; Syndication International 146 bottom.

Published by Country Life Books,
an imprint of The Hamlyn Publishing Group Limited,
Bridge House, 69 London Road, Twickenham, Middlesex, England TW1 3SB
and distributed for them by
Hamlyn Distribution Services Limited,
Rushden, Northants, England NN10 9RZ.

First published 1986
ISBN 0 600 33292 6
Printed in England

CONTENTS

AUTHOR'S ACKNOWLEDGEMENTS

I am indebted to many people for their generous help and cooperation in producing this book. Among those who gave me invaluable information about Lord Maclean are: His Royal Highness, The Prince of Wales, Dr. Robert Runcie, Archbishop of Canterbury, and the following, who appear in no particular order:

Lord Whitelaw, Sir Henry Clowes, Major General, Lord Michael Fitzalan Howard, Lord Home of the Hirsel, David Bankes, the late Col. J.L. Harvey, Sir Alistair Airde, Vice Admiral, Sir Peter Ashmore, Lord Elgin, The Right Reverend Michael Mann, Canon James Mansel, Canon Anthony Caesar, The Right Reverend Donald Coggan, Lt. Col. Sir John Miller, Sir Philip Moore, Lady Susan Hussey, Sir Oliver Millar, Lord Charteris of Amisfield, Dorien Belson, Capt. David Mellis, Mrs. Jeannie Maclean, Jim Smith, Penny Patrick, Sir Fitzroy Maclean, Rev. Allan Maclean, Mrs. Detta Maclean, Amanda Thomas, John Titman, Lt. Col. Sir John Johnston, Ken Stevens, Graham Coombe, Peter Cook, Charles Dymoke-Green, Charles Frazer, Major Jim Grant, Sir Eric Penn, John Mann and George Mann.

The Maclean family themselves have been extremely helpful in providing me with valuable background information about Lord Maclean and refreshingly honest in their anecdotes about him. David Graham-Campbell and his wife Joan (Lord Maclean's sister) were able and willing to fill in many details of Lord Maclean's early life, and also of the recent history of the family. The Hon. Lachlan Maclean spoke about his father, both as a parent and as Chief of the Clan, while Lord Maclean's daughter, the Hon. Mrs. Barne, was able to give me a fascinating insight into life at Duart, Holyroodhouse and St James's Palace.

And of course Lord and Lady Maclean themselves. They could not have been kinder and more cooperative, even as I delved deeper and deeper into their private lives. Their patience was inexhaustible and their hospitality ever generous. I regard it as a privilege to have been a guest in their homes on so many occasions – thank you. I would like to thank Ian Muggeridge for his excellent design of this book. Finally, as ever, I am grateful to Patricia Pierce for her usual skill in editing this book.

INTRODUCTION

Charles Hector Fitzroy Maclean, Baron Maclean of Duart and Morvern in the County of Argyll is 27th Chief of the Clan Maclean and as such, titular head of a family whose branches stretch from the Isle of Mull, off the west coast of Scotland, to the four corners of the world.

There are Macleans in New Zealand and Australia, throughout the South Seas and across the continents of Africa and Asia. There are more Macleans in the United States of America than there are in Scotland itself. *The Times* of 10th November, 1884, reported the death of Rear-Admiral Archibald Maclean, 'one of the most distinguished officers of the Imperial German Navy'; he was descended from those who fled to Europe after the Jacobite Rebellion. There are Dutch Macleans and even Japanese Macleans. And each one acknowledges as home the 13th-century Duart Castle, which sits brooding on its promontory overlooking and guarding the sea approaches from Oban.

This is where they come; those oil men from Dallas and those sheep farmers from Christchurch, and others bringing with them the accents of downtown Los Angeles and the harsh twang of the Australian outback. Itinerant clansmen all, seeking their roots and longing to prove that they belong to the family presided over by the jovial, stocky figure in tartan kilt, who greets them at the front door.

I was first given the idea of writing the life story of Lord Maclean when I was engaged in preparing a biography of Her Royal Highness, the Princess Anne. For a whole year I travelled the length and breadth of the United Kingdom in the wake of the Princess and one of the nicest occasions was when the Court was sitting at the Palace of Holyroodhouse in Edinburgh. I had been allowed to watch preparations for a Royal Garden Party, the organisation of which is always left in the capable hands of the Lord Chamberlain and his staff. At that time Charles Maclean occupied the exalted position as Head of the Queen's Household and I was able to observe at close quarters some of the qualities that had made him one of the most distinguished courtiers in modern times.

Even so, it was one of the Ladies-in-Waiting who suggested that he might be a good subject for a book when I had finished the project with Princess Anne. I would like to claim it was an original idea of my own – but it wasn't! This particular Lady told me that 'Chips' (the name by which he has been known since childhood and is called by everyone, even the Queen) had more stories to be told about himself than any other member of the Court. After all he was the man who had stage-managed more Royal ceremonial than any other, ranging from the funeral of the late Duke of Windsor (his was the figure seen escorting the fragile Duchess aboard the aircraft of The Queen's Flight as she returned to her home in Paris) to such splendid occasions as the weddings of Princess Anne and Captain Mark Philips and that of the Prince of Wales and Lady Diana Spencer. One of the most human and delightful scenes was when he was bidding farewell to the Royal couple as they boarded the Royal Train at Waterloo at the start of their honeymoon. As a spontaneous gesture of appreciation for all the hard work that had gone into making the day one of the most memorable in living history, the Princess of Wales kissed the Lord Chamberlain on the cheek, in the full view of the hundreds of millions of people who were watching the proceedings live on television throughout the world. Lord Maclean later described it as 'a lovely surprise'. Not all that many people can claim to have been kissed by a future Queen of England, in front of the largest audience in the world.

Lord Maclean's attention to detail is regarded as outstanding even in an organisation where such qualities are taken as a matter of course. During the funeral procession of Lord Mountbatten of Burma, he was seen to step out of line for an instant to straighten a banner which had fallen slightly awry, and to rearrange a wreath in danger of falling off the coffin.

In between arranging such Royal ceremonial as the Queen's Silver Jubilee celebrations, the annual Garden Parties at Buckingham Palace and Holyroodhouse and the funeral of the Duke of Gloucester, Lord Maclean during his term of office as Lord Chamberlain was also respon-sible for such disparate areas as the Royal works of art, the crown jewels, the Queen's swans and the Master of the Queen's Music, and duties such as the awarding of Royal Warrants, acting as Chancellor of the Royal Victorian Order (the Sovereign's personal order of chivalry) and explaining to foreign Heads of State, with consummate skill and unend-ing patience, the protocol to be observed when entertaining the Queen.

Lord Maclean was Lord Chamberlain from 1971 until his retirement in December 1984. Before his appointment to the Royal Household he was best known as Chief Scout of the Commonwealth, and perhaps best remembered by thousands of grateful young men as the man respon-sible for allowing them to replace the old, 'baggy shorts' of pre-Second World War days, with the more modern 'tapered' look of long trousers. He would perhaps wish to be remembered for many more positive achievements during his time as leader of the two million Scouts in the

Commonwealth, but that one single act earned more headlines than all the others put together, and the undying gratitude of a generation. I had the opportunity of seeing Sir Charles (as he then was) in action during a Scout jamboree in North Wales. There were more than 3,000 young men from all over the world present and Chips made sure he shook the hand of every single Scout. Perhaps it's just as well that Scouts use the left hand when greeting another member of the Movement.

Another memory I have of that particular occasion is the fact that Sir Charles, no matter how tired he must have felt, always managed to appear interested in everything that was going on in the camp, and he always seemed to have a smile on his face. Maybe that's the reason he was given a special name of 'Masekaseka' by Scouts at Gillfalls, near the Victoria Falls in what was then called Northern Rhodesia, now known as Zambia. 'Masekaseka' is the African term for 'the man who smiles'. Another name bestowed on him, this time by Scouts of Kaikohe in the Omapere District of New Zealand, is 'Kauri' the Maori name meaning 'Be Strong'. This refers to his unbounded physical energy and his spiritual strength, which many people who know him well, claim is the backbone of his entire existence. As a Christian he has never wavered in his belief and he is one of the few people I have met who goes to church every Sunday, not out of any sense of duty, but because he thoroughly enjoys it. As he once put it, 'There's only one thing wrong with Sunday; you have to wait a whole week for another one to come along.'

Charles Maclean is the personification of the Scouter's dream – the private soldier who actually did find the field marshal's baton in his knapsack. He was the first Chief Scout of the United Kingdom and the Commonwealth who started out as a Wolf Club, and it was as a school-boy Wolf Cub that he first met the man whose name became synonymous with the Movement he founded.

The young Maclean was on his way to visit his grandfather, the legendary Fitzroy Maclean who lived to be a hundred years old. On board the steamer to the Isle of Mull, they passed Duart Castle and Charles waved vigorously to the elderly gentleman who he knew was waiting in the castle. A man standing next to the youngster asked if he knew the person he was waving to. 'Oh, yes Sir,' said the boy, 'He's my grandfather.' The man then asked the boy his name. 'My name's Maclean, Sir, but my friends call me Chips.' The man replied, 'Well, my name is Baden-Powell, but my friends call me B-P.' An omen for the future perhaps? A meeting between someone who was already a legend in his own lifetime and a youngster on the threshold of a life that was to take him all over the world and place him as the Head of the Sovereign's Household.

In between would come a distinguished career as a soldier in the Scots

Guards with contemporaries such as Dr Robert Runcie, later to become Archbishop of Canterbury, and Willie Whitelaw, who was to go on to achieve great success in the world of politics as Home Secretary, and who is now, as Viscount Whitelaw, Leader of the House of Lords.

Born in 1916 when his father was serving also as a Major in the Scots Guards, Charles Maclean succeeded to the baronetcy on the death of his grandfather in 1936, his own father having died shortly after the First World War. He himself was only twenty-three when the second 'war to end all wars' was declared, and for him the brightest spot in the entire war came in 1941 when Sir Charles married Elizabeth, a member of the Mann brewing family, whose brother and father had each captained Middlesex and England at cricket. Lady Maclean has remained by his side ever since, even acting as stand-in for the Queen during the rehearsals for the Silver Jubilee Service in 1977. They have two children, a son Lachlan who followed his father and grandfather into the Scots Guards and reached the same rank, Major; and a daughter who, though married and now living in Norfolk, is still styled as The Maid of Morvern.

The Maclean family has a long-standing tradition of service to the Crown; the first baronet, Sir Lachlan, was an early and life-long supporter of Charles I. The present Chief of the Clan is very much a typical Highland Chief with an enviable record in public life. He has been Lord Lieutenant of the County of Argyll for more than thirty years and was Convenor of the Standing Council of Scottish Chiefs and President of the Highland Cattle Society. For five years from 1954 to 1959 he was Chief Commissioner of Scouts for Scotland and he remains as President of the Argyll Territorial Army Association and Lieutenant of the Royal Company of Archers – the Queen's personal bodyguard in Scotland.

In 1985 he represented the Queen for the second time as Lord High Commissioner of the General Assembly of the Church of Scotland, residing in great splendour in the State Apartments at the Palace of Holyroodhouse in Edinburgh during the eight days of the Assembly. When the time came for him to retire as Lord Chamberlain, Lord Maclean handed back to the Queen his white Wand of Office as tradition demands. Her Majesty returned it as a keepsake and also used the occasion to award her old friend the Royal Victorian Chain, one of the rarest honours bestowed by the Sovereign. Not only that, but the Queen was determined that she was not going to lose the services of one of her most loyal and trusted servants entirely. A few months after leaving St James's Palace Lord and Lady Maclean took up residence in Hampton Court Palace where he had been appointed Chief Steward as a reward for his years of service to the Crown.

Relieved of his day-to-day duties running the multitude of departments required to maintain the dignity of the monarchy, Lord Maclean is now able to return more often to life as a Scottish Chief. No more the 'absentee landlord' he feared he was becoming, he is able to devote more of his life to looking after the castle on the Isle of Mull and, more importantly in the view of many of those who live there permanently, to be seen to be in residence. The local people like to think that 'the Chief' is 'up there at the Castle' and when visitors from all over the world come to Duart, its important that they are greeted by the man they all know as the Head of the Clan. He's delighted if they drop in for tea. So this then is the 27th Chief of the Clan Maclean. Soldier, diplomat, farmer, Royal servant, church leader, Scout, Privy Councillor, author and above all, the most human of human beings – Charles Hector Fitzroy Maclean.

Chapter 1

LORD HIGH COMMISSIONER

The house guests at the Palace of Holyroodhouse in Edinburgh during the third week in May, 1985 were a fairly mixed bunch. There was the Duke and Duchess of Norfolk and the Tory rebel, Mr Francis Pym, the High Commissioner for the Kingdom of Swaziland and the Bishop of Bath and Wells. The Earl of Mar and Kellie brought his Countess while the Crown Equerry, Lt Col Sir John Miller, who's a bachelor, came alone, as did former Prime Minister Edward Heath. George Younger, Her Majesty's Secretary of State for Scotland, was there with Mrs Younger, and the Director General of the BBC, Alisdair Milne, sat down with the Spanish Ambassador and the Earl and Countess of Roseberry.

Princess Margaret's Equerry, Major the Lord Napier and Ettrick, arrived on the Tuesday along with the Surveyor of the Queen's Pictures, Sir Oliver Millar, the leader of the Liberal Party, Mr David Steel, and to add a little glamour to the gathering, the actor Anthony Andrews came with his wife Georgina. The dignified figure of the Lord Chief Justice rubbed shoulders with cricket commentator Brian Johnston and the Swiss Ambassador sat next of the Duchess of Argyll at dinner. The church was represented by the Moderator of the Church of Scotland, the Dean of the Chapel Royal and Canon James Mansel.

A mixture put together by the host and hostess for the week, Lord and Lady Maclean, with special and subtle regard for the protocol required when one is representing the Queen at her Scottish Palace.

For this was the week of the General Assembly of the Church of Scotland and Lord Maclean, former Lord Chamberlain, had been appointed by Her Majesty to be Lord High Commissioner and, as such, his was the premier position in the land for those eight glorious days. No one takes precedence over the Lord High Commissioner during the General Assembly. He is addressed by all as 'Your Grace' – in Scotland the Sovereign is held in ecclesiastical awe, and is always referred to in the same way as an Archbishop, though God forbid that the subject of Bishops in the 'Kirk' should arise yet again.

It was the second occasion that His Lordship had been honoured as Lord High Commissioner so he was well versed in the form that was required of him and Lady Maclean, for his wife also had an important role to place in the proceedings of the week. It must still have been a strange sensation to take control of a palace in which one had been a servant, albeit the most senior of servants, for more than thirteen years.

The week actually begins on Friday afternoon when the Macleans arrive to take up residence at the Palace of Holyroodhouse. Dinner promptly at 7.30 with twenty-eight sitting down in the Queen's Dining Room. Always the same number, twenty-eight, whether for lunch or dinner. Drinks before the meal in the gracious Drawing Room where each guest of whatever rank greets Their Graces with a bow or curtsey; a little formality which might not seem important to some but which is observed with meticulous attention by each and every guest, paying the Lord High Commissioner and his wife the same courtesy as would be paid to the Queen and her Consort. The Duke of Argyll finds it strange perhaps having to bow to the Chief of a clan that has been his own family's traditional enemy for centuries.

After dinner the first of the week's formal engagements, the Ceremony of the Keys. Whenever the Queen arrives in Scotland to take up residence in her Palace of Holyroodhouse, there is one small ceremony which always occurs on the day of her arrival. The Keys of the City are officially presented to Her Majesty by the Lord Provost. On this occasion Her Majesty's place is taken by the Lord High Commissioner who accepts the Keys and then returns them to the Lord Provost for safekeeping. It is a ceremony that is more than 300 years old, having been started for the first official visit to the city by King Charles I in 1646, and Lord Maclean is acutely aware of a sense of history as he takes part in this most delightful and unique formality.

Then a reception starting at 9.30 to which some 300 guests have been invited. Every one is received personally by the Macleans and His Lordship (or His Grace as he shall be known for the duration of this week) seems to have something to say to each one. Many of them he has met before, either as Lord Chamberlain, Lord High Commissioner or more probably when he was Chief Scout. This is where his legendary memory for names and faces is superbly demonstrated as each receives a word of friendly greeting and if they have met before, the occasion is always remembered by His Grace.

On Saturday it is raining. It is raining in Edinburgh and also a hundred miles away on the Isle of Mull, ancestral seat of the Clan Maclean.

Captain David Mellis RN (Retd) wakes early at his cottage on the seashore at Salen. As he looks out of his bedroom window he sees the early morning ferry for Tobermory steaming past and his experienced sailor's eye tells him that this is no ordinary spring shower – the rain is in for the day; which is a pity because today he's going to a Garden Party at the Palace of Holyroodhouse in Edinburgh.

Alistair and Susan Campbell are also up early, but then they usually are, for they live in a tiny house tucked under the main walls of Duart Castle and there's always plenty to do when you are the handyman, plumber, carpenter, bricklayer, mason and just about everything else to the Chief. But not today. They too are off to Edinburgh to mix with the generals and ambassadors, bishops and dukes.

It's something of a red-letter day throughout the island because the Chief has invited many of his old friends and family retainers to join him and Lady Maclean at the palace.

John and Penny Patrick run the island's only three-star hostelry, The Isle of Mull Hotel. But today somebody else will see to the menus, make sure the sheets have been changed and welcome the new coach party from England, because today someone will be waiting on them for a change. They are going to see what life is like in the capital city as honoured guests of the Lord High Commissioner of the Church of Scotland.

Jeannie Maclean and her husband Colum would like to be able to go too, but Jeannie has rheumatism and she is confined to her bed on this particular Saturday in her tiny croft now isolated since the new road has bypassed them. But she'll be there in spirit – and she has been a guest at St James's Palace after all.

There's only one way out of Mull and that's by sea. The first ferry of the day is at nine o'clock. And although it's raining hard the crossing which takes forty-five minutes is a calm one. Then once they have disembarked at Oban it's off on the long drive through the Highlands to Loch Awe, Crianlarich and Stirling before hitting the motorway which will carry them into the heart of the Scottish capital.

They arrive in Edinburgh at lunchtime, which gives them plenty of time to book into the hotel, change into best clothes ready for the afternoon which is due to start at three o'clock. The invitation has specified that dress is informal; that means no hiring of morning coats and top hats. But the ladies of the party have gone to great lengths to make sure that they are not outdone in their dresses and hats, some of which would not look out of place at Royal Ascot.

Meanwhile the day has started equally early back at Holyroodhouse. The Lord High Commissioner has attended his daily prayers at 8.15, then inspected the Guard of Honour lined up on the forecourt of the palace – he has to get used to the Royal Salute which is accorded him everytime he leaves or enters the palace, as opposed to the normal courtesy paid to every officer. Then at ten o'clock precisely there is the formal Opening of the General Assembly which is the official start of the most prestigious event in the Scottish calendar.

At one o'clock, luncheon with twenty-eight sitting down. The guests on this first Saturday include most of those who have to be invited because of their positions in Scottish life. The Moderator of the Church of Scotland and Mrs. Paterson, the Secretary of State for Scotland, the Dean of the Thistle, Scotland's oldest and most senior order of Chivalry. But as befits a Lord High Commissioner who is not himself a member of the Kirk (he's an Episcopalian), there is also the United Kingdom's leading lay Catholic, His Grace the Duke of Norfolk, to lend an ecumenical air to the proceedings. Luncheon is formal but relaxed, with Lord Maclean showing no sign of tension at the thought of the week that lies ahead. He is an urbane, considerate host, but well aware of the position he holds and nobody is left in any doubt about who is the Queen's representative. After lunch there's barely time to rest before the first of the 3,500 guests who have been invited to the Garden Party start to arrive. The invitation says three o'clock until 5.30 pm and most of them are determined to arrive at the beginning and remain until the end. It may well be the only occasion for most of them to have the chance of being inside the Palace of Holyroodhouse. It's still raining and umbrellas are very much the order of the day. There's a small queue to sign the Visitor's Book at the Garden Entrance and then those who know the form make a beeline for the ruins of the Abbey alongside the main house. That's because there are plenty of places to shelter among the ruins.

Although the invitations say 'informal dress', a number of the male guests have decided to wear tails and top hats. Overseas visitors are in national dress and there's a goodly supply of military uniforms on show with a fair sprinkling of kilts. The band of the Argyll and Sutherland Highlanders are on duty playing selections from 'My Fair Lady' and 'Oklahoma'. All the while a gentle drizzle comes down and here in the heart of Scotland's capital city, it's a somehow very English scene, with guests strolling around the beautiful gardens, overlooked by the splendour of Arthur's Seat, or sitting drinking tea and eating chocolate cake, ignoring the weather.

At four o'clock exactly the Lord High Commissioner attended by the Purse Bearer, Charles Fraser, and an Equerry from the Royal Marines walks through the doorway leading from the Royal Apartments. His path is cleared by his escort of High Constables, resplendent in their distinctive blue uniforms and cockaded silk bonnets which were approved by King George V in 1914. The Holyrood Constables are theoretically in charge of all security at the palace, but these days their function is almost entirely ceremonial. It is from their ranks that a Guard of Honour is selected to be on duty at all Royal and other formal occasions. And everything comes to a halt as the National Anthem is played.

Lady Maclean is attended by a number of Ladies-in-Waiting led by her daughter Janet who, although a married woman with two children, is still styled throughout Scotland as The Maid of Morvern – the daughter of the Chief.

Briefly the rain has stopped and the sun begins to appear. In any case, in Scotland the weather is something to be ignored – it's there all the time so why waste time commenting on it?

Lord Maclean moves at a steady pace through the assembled guests some of whom have been primed by his advance party to expect to be presented personally. If they've got a special reason for being invited or there's an entertaining story to be told, they stand a good chance of being chosen.

His Grace is wearing a kilt of Maclean Hunting Tartan with a tweed jacket and looks exactly as a Highland Chief should look: broad, upright and proud. The visitors from overseas in particular are crowding anxiously forward to catch a glimpse of their host. But there is no need to panic; 3,500 is a comfortable number to accommodate in the gardens of Holyroodhouse. When the Queen holds her annual Garden Party in July, the guest list runs to over 7,000.

More than an hour spent mingling with his guests and pausing to offer a word of thanks to the Band of the Argyll and Sutherland Highlanders, the Macleans return to the terrace outside the entrance to the Private Apartments. Once again the National Anthem is played and while the ladies and gentlemen on the lawns settle down to enjoy the tea or iced coffee and cucumber sandwiches and cakes, Their Graces move back inside the palace to the Equerries Room. They are followed at a discreet distance by a small party. These are the special guests from Mull; the old friends, some of whom have worked for Lord Maclean for decades and they are going to take their tea with Their Graces in the splendour of Holyroodhouse itself. It's a pleasant and generous gesture on the part of the hosts. They do not get very many opportunities to offer such unique hospitality to old friends and family retainers and they are obviously delighted to be able to share their good fortune on this special occasion.

It's been a long day for some of those who have travelled more than a hundred miles on sea and land, and the unaccustomed constrictions of collars and ties are beginning to make themselves felt, so as well as the tea and cakes on offer, 'a wee dram' goes down a treat. Lord Maclean is famous for the size of his 'wee drams' and very soon the atmosphere becomes relaxed and friendly with the soft brogues of the Western Isles mixing easily with the sophisticated tones of the Home Counties.

However there is one notable abstainer, His Grace himself. He doesn't drink whisky, although this might be construed as heresy in a man who is truly a Highland Chief – and a director of the mighty Distiller's Company, the world's largest manufacturers of Scotland's major product. Neither does he drink tea or coffee. Coffee he simply doesn't care for, and he hasn't tasted tea for more than sixty years since his sister Joan chased him around the nursery with a tea cosy and succeeded in forcing his face into it for what must have seemed like an eternity. From such childish innocent experiences are life-time phobias developed. Nevertheless tea, coffee and whisky are out, but a glass of milk or beer is always welcome.

Once the private family guests have been entertained there is a further duty call to be made by His Grace before the afternoon is out. He traditionally is invited to visit the High Constables Mess in the Palace, there to thank them for their attention throughout the Garden Party. This is a convivial duty; most of the members of this Honourable Company are old friends and while they observe the courtesy of greeting him as 'Your Grace' as custom demands, in private they all know him as 'Chips' his nickname from the day he was born.

Sunday sees the most splendid of all the week's formalities, the Assembly Service in the High Kirk of Edinburgh, St Giles Cathedral. Shortly before the service begins Lord Maclean inspects the Guard of Honour provided by the Boys Brigade drawn up in Parliament Square. It's raining heavily but this hasn't deterred the hundreds of onlookers, most of whom appear to be Americans, who have come to witness one of the most spectacular processions to be seen in the Scottish capital.

The procession is led by Heralds and Pursuivants in their colourfully embroidered tabards.

Next comes the Hereditary Bearer of the Flag of St Andrew, the Earl of Lauderdale, and the Hereditary Bearer of the Standard of Scotland, the Earl of Dundee.

Also in attendance are the Earl of Erroll and the Duke of Argyll as Hereditary Lord High Constable and Hereditary Master of the Household in Scotland respectively, both of whom are included in the House Party during the week.

The Lord High Commissioner and Lady Maclean enter the cathedral singing the Processional Hymn: 'Praise my soul, the King of Heaven' – and neither has the need to seek the assistance of the hymn sheet for the words. The Purse Bearer, Charles Fraser, precedes the Lord High Commissioner as he would the Sovereign if she were present. St Giles is packed with every pew filled and an overspill being seated in the aisles and even the empty spaces at the back of the church full of those members of the public who have managed to get in without an invitation. There is a small gallery which has been reserved for the Lord High Commissioner's private party. Three rows of seats alongside the Royal

Pews. As Lord Maclean takes his seat he bows to the congregation and the three Heralds, Albany, Marchmont and Rothesay, and the three Pursuivants, Carrick, Kintyre and Unicorn take their places facing the Lord High Commissioner. Then the congregation also face the Royal Pews during the National Anthem.

The four ministers of the Kirk complete the procession, The Right Reverend David Smith, Moderator of the General Assembly; The Reverend Ronald Blakey, Senior Chaplain to the Moderator; The Reverend David Clark, Junior Chaplain; and the Minister of St Giles itself, The Reverend Gilleasbuig Macmillan.

The cathedral is Edinburgh's most historic church. Dedicated as a parish church in 1243, it was here that John Knox thundered out his sermons of hell and damnation as its first Protestant minister and it was here that Mary, Queen of Scots attended worship with all the attendant splendour of her Parliament. And the cathedral is also the religious home of the Most Ancient and Most Noble Order of the Thistle whose chapel, measuring just thirty-three feet by seventeen feet was designed by Sir Robert Lorrimer in 1909. The Chapel contains nineteen stalls. One for the Sovereign, two for other members of the Royal Family and sixteen for the Knights who form this most exclusive order of chivalry. The Lord High Commissioner as Sir Charles Maclean of Duart and Morvern was installed as a Knight of the Thistle on Monday, 26th May, 1969 in the presence of Her Majesty the Queen, the Duke of Edinburgh and Queen Elizabeth, the Queen Mother. Morning service on this opening Sunday of the General Assembly lasts just over an hour and the crowds have thickened along the Royal Mile as the State Procession leaves the Cathedral for the short journey back down the steep hill to the Palace of Holyroodhouse where a further twenty-eight guests are invited for luncheon.

On Sunday afternoon the Lord High Commissioner is due to pay a visit to a children's tea party held in the Palace where forty high-spirited and excitable youngsters, who are not in the least intimidated by the rank of their exalted visitor, ply him with questions, or ignore him completely if the game they are playing is too engrossing.

It's back to business after the tea party as the official limousines carry the Lord High Commissioner and his escorts to the Assembly Hall to listen to the Moderator's Address – not always the most stimulating way to spend the early part of Sunday evening, but nonetheless one of the required duties to be carried out by a diligent Lord High Commissioner before yet another official dinner party at the palace.

The working week proper begins at 8.15 on Monday morning with Household prayers, followed by Assembly Communion Service and Their Graces remain at the Assembly until nearly one o'clock.

The General Assembly of the Church of Scotland is the nearest thing that Scotland has to a national assembly, following the cessation of the Scottish Parliament after the Act of Union in 1707. The importance of the General Assembly cannot be overestimated, hence the appointment by the Queen of a Lord High Commissioner to represent her for this one event only, if she does not attend. She has, in fact, attended once, in 1969, the first time since the Reformation that a reigning monarch has done so.

But although the Lord High Commissioner takes precedence over all others and makes a speech from the Throne in the Assembly Hall, he takes no other part in the proceedings or the business of the Assembly. The Sovereign's representative sits with his party in the Throne Gallery at the back of the hall, but he is required to remain silent during the discussions. In Scotland spiritual matters are not considered to be part of the Crown's province!

So throughout the week, while delegates to the Assembly debate the burning issues of the day, Lord and Lady Maclean undertake a large number of outside official engagements, some jointly, others independently. On one afternoon they both visit the Aberfoyle Scottish Conservation Projects Trust and later Queen's Bay Lodge, one of the Church of Scotland's homes for retired ministers. There is one mild criticism of a proposed visit to Glasgow to see the Stirling Maxwell Collection at Pollok House and the nearby Burrell Collection. Criticism which is stilled when Lord Maclean gently points out that it is the General Assembly of the Church of *Scotland* and not just Edinburgh. Then they split up, Lady Maclean to travel to the Princess Margaret Rose Hospital and His Grace to visit the Royal Hospital for Sick Children. He goes to Leith to see the Urban Renewal Programme and she goes to the Women's Guild and the Victoria League. All the time fitting in sittings for official photographs within the palace, and the ever present luncheons, dinners, receptions and being present for at least part of the day at the Assembly itself.

Perhaps it's because there are so many official calls upon His Grace's time, and so many guests who have to be offered hospitality because of their position in Scottish life, that Lord Maclean has 'sweetened the pill' a little by including a number of guests who are old friends, with no particular claim to an official invitation. Men such as Canon James Mansel, former Chaplain to the Queen and one time sub-Dean of the Chapels Royal, now retired and living in North London. This is also why Lady Jean Rankin, one of Her Majesty, Queen Elizabeth, the Queen Mother's Ladies-in-Waiting, also finds herself on the guest list for the same evening. When Chips and Elizabeth lived at St James's Palace, Lady Jean was just across the road in Clarence House and they were frequent guests at each other's parties. Lady Norrie is another member of the family who's come to stay. She is the daughter of Lady Maclean's younger brother John who now lives in America.

Lt Col Sir John Johnston is Comptroller of the Lord Chamberlain's Office – the man who actually is in charge on a day-to-day basis. Tall, good looking – the personification of a British Guards officer (he's a Grenadier), he is also one of the easiest people in the world to get along with and having worked alongside Lord Maclean for several years knows the stresses and strains that public office can impose – so he too is a welcome guest with whom His Grace can 'let his hair down'.

Sir Oliver Millar is Surveyor of the Queen's Pictures, responsible for more than 5,000 paintings in the Royal Collection. An intellectual and tremendous enthusiast, his presence would grace any gathering.

Lt Col Sir John Miller is the Crown Equerry, which means he is responsible for all the horses, carriages and motor cars in the Royal Mews. He's been at Buckingham Palace for more than a quarter of a century and probably knows the Queen better than any of her Household (with the possible exception of Bobo Macdonald her dresser). His interests are mainly equestrian and certainly to do with the countryside. He likes to hunt, shoot and fish, none of which appeals in the slightest to his host at Holyroodhouse. But this has never been a bar to their friendship. They first met when they were both in the Brigade of Guards; Chips in the Scots Guards (of course) and John Miller in the Welsh Guards. An immediate rapport was established and they have remained firm friends ever since.

And so when all the formal functions have been completed and the last official guest has departed, Chips is able to sit in the elegant drawing room surrounded by family and close friends and reflect on his week as Lord High Commissioner.

As he looks around the room he is able to look back with some satisfaction on an outstandingly successful week. Everybody who should have been invited has been included, there have been no major catastrophes – even the weather perked up a little towards the end. And how does he sum it all up?

Turning to Johnnie Johnston he says 'Isn't this all marvellous fun?' And perhaps that's the secret of his own remarkable success. Although he is dutiful to a fault, he finds joy in everything he does. He is never bored and rarely discontent. His ever present sense of humour gets him through experiences which would be stultifying if he couldn't see the funny side of life. On the most solemn of occasions a slight gleam in his eye can sometimes be detected.

This has been one week in the life of Lord Maclean, a life that began seventy years ago in the middle year of the First World War.

Chapter 2

THE EARLY YEARS

Friday, 5th May, 1916 was a bright, sunny, beautiful English spring day. It was also the day on which some 82 British officers and 293 other ranks were listed as killed in France. For this of course, was the time of the First World War; almost in fact the halfway point, when the Allied Forces had been at war with Germany for twenty months. HMS *Russell*, one of His Majesty's warships, had been sunk with the loss of 94 men, but 663 had been saved in an heroic action.

The Times reported that The Military Service Bill, introduced to bring conscription to the country because the supply of volunteers was drying up, had received its Second Reading in the House of Commons with Mr Lloyd George, eloquent and passionate as ever, in a speech supporting the bill, claiming that it could mean the difference between victory and defeat. Newspapers also reported on the introduction of something called 'The Daylight-Saving Bill' which meant that habits of a lifetime would be altered and clocks and watches put back an hour during the long summer days in order that vital energy needed for the war effort would be saved.

The Court Circular of the day reported that King George V inspected his troops on Salisbury Plain and Prince Albert left Windsor Castle to rejoin his ship with the Fleet, while the young Prince George returned to school at St Peter's Court, Broadstairs. Princess Alexander of Teck dined with the King and Queen, Prince Cantacuzene of Rumania arrived at Claridges and Lord Rothschild was in residence at the Empire Hotel, Bath. It was the anniversary of the death of King Edward VII and Mr Fred Terry 'is going on very well.'

Dame Clara Butt performed two new war works by Sir Edward Elgar, and Charles Hawtry and Gladys Cooper were at The Playhouse in 'Please Help Emily'.

In Paris the Hotel Lutetia offered 'special arrangements for officers for the duration' and the Ritz took a large advertisment in the English papers to announce that it was remaining open throughout the war.

Back in London there was an air of excited expectancy at No 9 Gerald Road SW1. Madam was expecting her third child and it was due at any time. The master, Major Hector Maclean of the Scots Guards, was at home, on leave from his regiment, trying very hard to concentrate on his hobby, his collection of military medals. In the nursery seven-year-old

21

Joan was dying to know how things were going in the main bedroom below and even Donald, who though not yet three years old, was aware that something exciting was going to happen, but he wasn't quite sure what it was.

The hustle and bustle as nurses and maids hurried to and from the mistress's bedroom added to the excitement and it was a great relief when an infant cry was heard and one of the housemaids ran upstairs to announce that 'the mistress has had a baby boy.'

The children were taken down to see their brother and they were delighted to see that he had been born with a mop of bright red hair. His name had already been decided. It was to be Charles Hector Fitzroy Maclean and one of the early visitors was a regimental comrade of Major Maclean's named Carpenter-Garnier. With a surname like Carpenter he was inevitably called Chips by everyone. He took one look at the infant Charles and turning to Major Maclean said, 'He's certainly a chip off the old block.' From that moment Charles became 'Chips' and that he has remained ever since.

Meanwhile there was also a sense of anticipation on the Isle of Mull off the west coast of Scotland. Sir Fitzroy Maclean, 26th Chief of the Clan had just taken up residence at Duart Castle after its four-year restoration, and together with Lady Maclean he was waiting to hear whether he had another grandson or granddaughter. Jeannie Macleod was seven years old and was sitting in the tiny classroom at Lochdon Village School when there was a flurry of activity outside the window and they all saw the postman going by on his bicycle. And he was waving a telegram in his hand. For most people in Britain at this time a telegram meant only one thing – bad news from the front about a loved one. But not today. They all realised from his expression that it was the good news they were waiting for. The postman cycled the three miles from the village to the castle to deliver the news that another heir to the Macleans had been born. Sir Fitzroy was so pleased that he gave the postman a ninepenny tip – a handsome gift to a man whose weekly wage was less than a pound. Jeannie Macleod, she's now Mrs Calum Maclean, is in her late seventies and she worked at Duart for more than fifty years after leaving school, but she has total recall of that day in 1916, and remembers there was great rejoicing in the village, 'and if it hadn't been for the war we would have let off fireworks.'

Chips was a happy child in every way, sunny by nature and a loving brother and son. As he grew older he spent most of his time out of doors whenever he could. The house at Gerald Road was next door to the police station, said to be the prettiest police station in London, but one of the most frequent sights they witnessed was of drunks being carted off to the cells on Saturday nights. Chips recalls that they used to be strapped to trolleys 'rather like those at Waterloo Station', in very much the same way that porters would load trunks, and then wheeled singing and shouting through the police station to the cells at the back which were actually immediately adjacent to the nursery. Some years later this was mentioned as one of the reasons why Mrs Maclean decided that they should move house. As the children became older and more aware, she was concerned that they should not hear bad language emanating from the cells on Saturday nights.

But in those early days they lived side by side amicably and Major Maclean was an ardent supporter of the Annual Police Sports Day. Another neighbour in Gerald Road was a young man who spent most of his time playing the piano. As the Maclean children were taken on walks past his house they would see him sitting in the window of No 17 with a faraway look on his face, no doubt dreaming of stardom to come – and it wasn't many years before Noel Coward became a household name throughout the world.

The Maclean children were very much children of the nursery. They spent their time in the charge of Nurse Justice, a formidable, old-fashioned traditionalist whose word was law. Chips remembers that there was never any question of disobeying Nurse Justice and on the subject of food there was simply no discussion at all. 'We were required to eat everything that was put in front of us. The idea of refusing to eat something just because we didn't like it, didn't occur. We wouldn't have dared to leave anything on the plate with Nurse Justice watching our every move.' It was a fairly small household by the standards of the day: nurse, nursery maid, cook, housemaid and parlourmaid. At four o'clock every afternoon the children were washed and brushed to be taken down to the drawing room to see their parents for an hour, and to play with their special dressing-up box and toy Noah's Ark, before being returned upstairs to the care of the nursery staff. The young Chips was indeed a chip off the old block. He resembled his father in many ways, being unusually neat and methodical for a child, qualities he had certainly inherited from his father, who was also a very kind man, devoted to his family and to his regiment. Maclean senior had been educated at Eton and Sandhurst before being commissioned into the Scots Guards in February 1896 and seeing active service in the Boer War in South Africa in 1900 to 1901 when he was involved in the battles of Biddulphsberg and Wittebergen, being awarded the Queen's South Africa Medal with four clasps.

He was posted to Egypt for two years immediately before the outbreak of hostilities in 1914 and then, because of his age, he was forty-one when war was declared, he served for most of the early part of the war in the United Kingdom before being sent to France in 1918.

Major Maclean's over-riding passion was his regiment, its history and achievements, and he was regarded as one of the outstanding authorities on the Scots Guards. A keen piper, his principal off duty occupation was his collection of medals awarded to members of the regiment, which he traced and acquired, each one being documented with meticulous accuracy. The collection, which numbers several hundred all told, is now on permanent display at Regimental Headquarters in Wellington Barracks. He had married Chips' mother, Winifred Joan Wilding in 1907, at St Michael's Chester Square and eighteen months later their first child, a daughter Joan, was born in April 1909, followed four years later by Donald in 1913, and Chips in 1916.

After the birth of Donald, Mrs Maclean was never fully fit. It was discovered that she was suffering from a heart condition which meant that she needed a great deal of rest and remained confined to her room for much of the time. But this was no professional invalid who revelled in her ill health. She was one of the most cheerful people around and insisted in being included in all the family activities, even to the extent of going on family picnics (a favourite outing for the Major) by using a wheelchair, which made her very popular with her children, who thought it great sport to help push their mother along.

Her bedroom became a focal point for a great deal of activity in the Maclean household and as the children grew older, their friends would often be brought upstairs to tell Mrs Maclean all the latest gossip and to show off their fashionable clothes before a party or ball.

As a very small boy Chips remembers being taken to see his grandfather, the elderly Sir Fitzroy Maclean, at his grand house across the park at 15, Hyde Park Terrace. 'I was dressed in a kilt and silk shirt and had to suffer the catcalls of the town urchins who used to wait along the Bayswater Road in those days', he says.

Another early memory of those far-off days is that when the family went to visit grandfather they had to cross Bayswater Road from Hyde Park. There were not all that many motor cars around at the time, but there were still plenty of horses; at the point where one crossed the road there was always a man, known as a crossing sweeper, ready to clear the manure from the road so that one might cross freely. For this service he was rewarded with a ha'penny tip.

Grandfather's house in Hyde Park Terrace was a huge building complete with full-size ballroom, but as Chips remembers it 'most of the furniture seemed to be covered with dust sheets.' Chips cannot remember his grandfather as anything other than an old man – he was eighty when Chips was born, and it was from the year of Chips' birth – 1916 – that he gradually moved more and more to Duart as the ancient Castle was restored, following his purchase of it in 1911.

The Lord Chamberlain and Lady Maclean in their apartment at
St James's Palace before leaving to attend a State banquet. Lord
Maclean's decorations include the insignia of a Knight of the
Thistle and the Grand Cross of the Royal Victorian Order.

The Banquetting Hall at Duart has walls nine feet thick. The fireplace incorporates the Coat of Arms of the present Chief, and the three flags are the regimental colours of the 236th Battalion, Canadian Expeditionary Force, the Maclean Kilties of America.

The State Bedroom. The coverings were made specially for Lord Maclean and his young bride, Elizabeth, when they spent their honeymoon at Duart during the Second World War. The handsome writing-bureau once belonged to William Wordsworth.

After some persuasion, Lord and Lady Maclean agreed to allow television cameras into Duart for the BBC series 'Our House'. The programme, from which this still photograph was taken, was transmitted in November, 1984.

Undoubtedly the best way to view Duart Castle is from the sea and what better ship to see it from than the Royal Yacht, *Britannia* – this photograph was taken during one of *Britannia's* summer cruises off the Western Isles.

Three generations of Macleans serving the Queen. Lord Maclean in his robes as a Knight of the Thistle, his son, the Hon. Lachlan Maclean dressed as Adjutant of the Royal Company of Archers (the Sovereign's Personal Bodyguard in Scotland), and grandson Malcolm – a Page of Honour.

Life was comfortable for the Maclean family after the end of the First World War, and Major Maclean left the army in 1921 on medical grounds; he had contracted pleurisy during his time in Egypt and never fully recovered. So he was able to devote even more of his time to his medal collection and he retired even more into the seclusion of his library. He was a very private man, but paradoxically also an extremely happy head of the family. He enjoyed to the full family outings and parties, especially when they went to Mull or Oban in Scotland, or more frequently, to the house they owned at Folkestone in Kent.

One memory that remains clear in Chips' mind of those days, was that when they went to Folkestone, their luggage was delivered to the station in a van driven by a Mr Waters, whose daughters, Elsie and Doris, were soon to become famous throughout the land as the music hall comediennes, Gert and Daisy.

Because of Mrs Maclean's ill health, Chips' sister Joan assumed a great deal of responsibility for the youngest member of the family, even though she was only seven years older herself. That responsibility grew with the years and Chips relied more and more on Joan as they matured. Elder brother Donald was a Wolf Cub who attended meetings in Chester Square, until tragedy struck the family in May, 1923. Donald contracted meningitis, a fearful disease for which, at that time, there was little treatment available and which usually proved fatal. Such was the case with Donald. After a short illness, he died at the age of nine and a half. It was a devastating blow to the family. Donald had been a healthy youngster with an enormous appetite for life, and as the eldest son he was the natural successor to the baronetcy which was expected to come to his father in the course of time.

All this had now changed and Chips, the younger son, who in the normal course of events would have inherited nothing, was now the eventual heir to a fortune, and an ancient title.

Shortly after Donald's death the family moved from Gerald Road. Mother said that it was because of the bad language the children could hear from the police station next door, but probably the association with Donald's memory was too poignant and this obviously became a contributing factor.

So the family moved to a much larger house at 56, Cadogan Place, a magnificent town house in the heart of Belgravia, where the staff was expanded to include a cook, kitchen maid, housemaid, house parlour-maid and a butler plus a resident nurse who was engaged to look after Mrs Maclean.

Chips was enrolled at Mr Gibbs' preparatory school and a schoolroom was established in the house under the direction of Miss Alice Pickup who became their first governess. She was the daughter of a clergyman and her responsibilities were to supervise their meals, make sure their clothes were in order and to take them to school and collect them afterwards. Miss Pickup did not give lessons apart from the usual instruction in manners and etiquette and supervising homework.

At school Chips was an enthusiastic but not always successful amateur boxer. One of his early opponents, Dorien Belson, who later became chairman of Justerini and Brooks, one of Britain's leading wine importers, remembers meeting him in the ring over three rounds when they were about nine years old. 'I managed to beat him on points,' he says, 'but only after we had both suffered bloody noses.'

It was a privileged way of life enjoyed by comparatively few families in England at the time, but even then, and at such a tender age, Chips and his sister were aware of the poverty that surrounded them. 'As we were taken to school,' he recalls, 'we often saw barefoot children playing in the streets, but it seemed perfectly natural. I thought they were barefoot because they wanted to be, not because they simply didn't have shoes or stockings, but Joan always pointed out that they were too poor to buy shoes and that we were lucky.'

Chips' parents may well have been 'comfortably well off', but there was no evidence of an abundance of money in the household. Chips says: 'We didn't have a motor car in those days, even though there were a number in our road and grandfather had a gigantic Daimler at Duart which was fully five feet high, and as far as treating the servants was concerned, our parents were very strict. They were to be treated with respect by we children at all times and there was no question of us running to mother or father if they disciplined us – that was the order of the day.' Pocket money was doled out on Saturday mornings, three pence in old money a week. This was used at the shop on the corner to buy Comic Cuts and sweets, with usually one penny saved.

Chips showed a leaning towards music from an early age. He learnt to play the piano and violin, and then discovered he could also play by ear which later made him a very popular guest at parties. Much later in life, when he was Lord Chamberlain, his love of music was frequently demonstrated when he interested himself in the choice of music for Royal occasions and he showed a remarkable knowledge of sacred music, to the surprise and occasional delight of a number of Deans of the Chapels Royal, and even some of the organists.

When he was twelve years old Chips fell in love. He had been allowed to attend weekly ice-skating lessons at Grosvenor House in Park Lane, and while he was there one Saturday morning, he saw a young lady of about the same age with whom he immediately became smitten. Her name was Bobbie Tagg and when Chips discovered where she lived he used to walk past her house in the hope of seeing her. But the shyness of a twelve-year-old prevented him from declaring his feelings to her face, so he pinned a letter addressed to her on the notice board at Grosvenor House Ice-Rink, until his sister gently reminded him that a gentleman would never display a lady's name for all to see. The letter was removed and sadly the love of a young swain went unrequited and indeed unnoticed.

But other friendships blossomed, particularly when the family went on holiday to Duart Castle. The handyman at the castle, Mr Macleod, had come to the Isle of Mull a few years before the First World War from his home town of Glasgow, because his wife needed the fresh air. He had four young children, one of whom, Jeannie, was just a few years older than Chips. And with the innocence of youth and because no one had told them there was such a thing as class distinction, they all played happily together whenever the Maclean family came to Duart. Jeannie remembers that they kept their only pairs of shoes for Sundays; the rest of the week they ran barefoot. It wasn't long before Chips realised what he had been missing and frequently his shoes and stockings disappeared so that he could join in the fun and games. Jeannie Maclean (as she now is) remembers the fearsome reputation of 'the old Chief', as she called Sir Fitzroy Maclean. He was an aloof, frightening figure to a young girl, particularly when he wore his regimental cloak, a relic from the Crimea, which was intended to cover 'man and beast'. And Sir Fitzroy was the only person who absolutely refused to use his grandson's nickname. If he heard any of the other youngsters calling him Chips, he was down on them in an instant, insisting that his name was Charles and that is what he was to be called. Jeannie recalls: 'If we saw him coming we kept well out of his way. In fact the only person who wasn't afraid of him was Chips himself.'

So although Chips was a Londoner born and bred, he was never left in any doubt about where his roots lay. 'I don't think it was impressed on me from an early age that I was a Maclean or indeed that to be a Maclean was anything special. But I was aware that I was a little Scots boy. I used to stand out at children's parties as the only little boy wearing a kilt.' Not a distinction that was always welcomed by a youngster in his formative years.

As the children grew older, Chips' sister Joan assumed more and more responsibility for the running of the house. She was an early recruit in the Girl Guides and the practical training she received at their hands served her well in the years to come. When he was eleven Chips was sent away to school to Beechborough Park in Kent and then on to public school. Although his father and grandfather had both been educated at Eton it was decided that Chips would not follow them, but would instead go to Canford in Dorset. Canford is a comparatively small public school, a former home of the Wimbourne family, and it was chosen because of its location in the middle of the country which would be beneficial because Chips had suffered rheumatic fever some years earlier. Chips' parents felt that after living in London it would do him good to get some healthy fresh air. There was another reason. To get into Canford it was not necessary to sit the Common Entrance examination which most public schools demanded. Chips admits that he was never at his best with examinations and the system at Canford was that the Headmaster, the Rev. C B Canning, interviewed all prospective pupils personally to see if they would fit in. He was more interested in character than academic achievement and subsequent events, in Chips' case at least, have proved him right.

Anyway Chips passed the interview test and was enrolled as a boarder. He took to Canford immediately – and Canford took to him. He made friends easily and his happy-go-lucky nature gave him a popularity that was envied. He did just enough to get by as regards his academic subjects – never outstanding, but always around the middle of the class. These days Chips claims he has always been 'a rabbit' at games, but friends from those far-off days at Canford remember him as an enthusiastic member of the rugby team and a more than proficient boxer. He was captain of squash racquets and played royal tennis – Canford is one of the few schools in England with a royal (or real) tennis court. He also played the violin in the school orchestra, though not from choice. Although he had learnt to play the violin at home, the lessons were dull and consequently he never came to regard the instrument with the same affection he felt for the piano. Which was a pity in some ways because there were plenty of competent pianists around Canford at the time, so Chips never achieved his ambition of playing in the school dance band, which was what he really wanted.

His housemaster was a renowned scholar and raconteur named Tom Nash, who said some years after Chips left school, that he was always happy to have him sitting next to him at dinner because he was never at a loss for something to say. Chips apparently was not in the least bit intimidated in the presence of adults and because of his enquiring mind he was prepared to talk about anything and everything. And it was while he was at Canford that his lifelong interest in church and the Christian way of life began to manifest itself.

He attended confirmation classes which were held in the open air on fine spring evenings, where they sometimes sat on tombstones and the church wall. And when the time came for him to be confirmed, although his mother was too ill to attend, Joan was there.

Joan is now Mrs David Graham-Campbell the wife of a retired housemaster at Eton and later warden of Trinity College, Glenalmond in

Perthshire. They live in a beautiful granite house in Scotland's ancient and former capital city of Perth, overlooking North Inch Park with an unobstructed view of the River Tay from their garden. The drawing room features a handsome painting of Joan's and Chips' mother which was commissioned in 1902 on the occasion of her engagement to Major Maclean.

Joan remembers travelling from the London house to Canford whenever it was necessary to fulfill her substitute parental duties, including the confirmation service, but she doesn't recall her brother being particularly religious at the time. She says, 'He certainly wasn't a goody-goody.' But Chips himself regards Canford as the starting point in his interest in church. He enjoyed chapel and frequently took house prayers when he became a prefect.

In July 1932 Chips' father died. He had been in poor health since the end of the First World War and indeed he never fully recovered from the illness he contracted in Egypt twenty years earlier. And although he was the most private of men, he was devoted to his family and his death was keenly felt by all of them. It also meant that at the age of sixteen Chips was now his grandfather's heir and would be required to accept the mantle of responsibility in a very few years. Old Sir Fitzroy Maclean was already in his late nineties and remained at Duart Castle throughout the year, for the remainder of his life.

But as a sixteen year old, still at school, the significance of those imminent responsibilities still seemed far off in 1932. Although his compassion was beginning to make itself felt even at that tender age. His sister remembers one incident which perhaps gives an illuminating insight into the character that was already forming. During a particularly cold winter when they were at home in Cadogan Place, the coalman was delivering the weekly fuel supply. Chips had been delegated to count the bags going into the cellar, and he became concerned about the appearance of the coalman, saying he looked too ill to be doing such heavy work. So he decided to give him an extra large tip. Afterwards Chips turned to Joan and said, 'I expect he has a good wife and family to care for him – I certainly hope so.' Perhaps not the expected reaction of a sixteen-year-old member of an upper-class household in the 1930s, but a foretaste of the sort of feeling he would show many times in later life.

One of the lessons Chips enjoyed particularly at Canford was German, mainly because there was a young, very capable German national as teacher. Chips remembers him taking the class to Germany on a couple of occasions 'to see the country and learn the language. One of the most impressive sights was the troops of the Hitler Youth marching around in their smart uniforms and highly polished boots. I remember thinking how well they compared with our Officer Training Corps back at school, much more military in their bearing. But we didn't have a great deal to do with them ourselves; they were just around all the time.' Of course this was a time when Germany was rearming and preparing for war, while the rest of the world preferred to ignore what was going on under the Nazi leader's direction.

In 1934 Chips left Canford to embark on his adult life. Although no clear pattern had emerged in the final years at school as far as his future career, he had always taken it for granted that he would eventually join his father's regiment, the Scots Guards and continue the family tradition. But before that decision had to be taken there was the exciting prospect of a world tour. In those days boys who had left, or were about to leave English public schools, were offered the opportunity of visiting the Empire to see for themselves just how widespread British possessions were, and to show them some of the opportunities available to young men on the threshold of their adult lives.

Chips joined a public schools' tour to Australia, after persuading his mother that the £148 return fare would be well spent. On board the ss *Orontes*, one of Orient's ocean-going liners, they set sail due east on the month-long voyage through the Suez Canal, across the Bay of Bengal, south of Singapore and down through the Pacific Ocean to Australia where the boys were given a true insight into almost every aspect of life in Australia. They were accommodated in homes which represented a virtual cross-section of life. Chips remembers staying in a very poor home belonging to the family of a miner on the outskirts of Calgoorlie in the Australian goldfields. 'The people were also pure gold,' he recalls. Then by complete contrast three of the boys, Chips included, were lodged in the Governor-General's residence in Canberra. They weren't chosen because of their connections, indeed, none of the boys or their families had met His Excellency before the visit; he simply sent his name in with all the other families who had offered accommodation, and took potluck as to who he would get. Chips remembers that some of the homes were very humble indeed, and conditions in some of the areas of the 'outback' at that time were primitive in the extreme, but the hospitality was universally warm and friendly, and he recalls: 'There was a tremendously pro-British feeling throughout Australia in the 1930s. Everywhere we went we were given a marvellous welcome by the people who were our hosts. They could not have been more generous if we had been their own sons.'

One establishment which made a great impression on Chips was Fairbridge Farm Schools in Western Australia. This organisation existed to give homes to immigrant children from Dr Barnado's orphanages. The boys were trained for jobs on the land, while the girls, in the main, went into domestic service. They did such a wonderful job for these underprivileged youngsters that Chips wanted to do something to help when he returned to England. He went to Western Australia House to offer his services as a volunteer helper for Fairbridge Farm Schools, only to be told that they already had plenty of assistance thank you very much. So his first attempts at public service, though well intended, came to naught.

But in the meantime the tour of Australia continued for five months during which time he saw almost every part of that vast country, with travel between cities and towns in many cases taking days, rather than hours.

Finally the time for the return journey to England came, and this time the boys were to travel the western route on the New Zealand ship *Ranoi Tata*, sailing across the South Pacific, through the Panama Canal and home across the Atlantic to Southampton. It had been the experience of a lifetime and for Chips his first glimpse of what was to become his 'parish' in years to come – the Commonwealth.

Back home it was decided that Chips needed some work experience before deciding what sort of career he was to pursue, so he went to the Royal Empire Society in Northumberland Avenue, where his first task was to put pamphlets into envelopes and stick on stamps. This naturally palled after a while and then came what he describes as his 'first real job'. 'My sister had a friend named Rupert Warburton who owned a factory near the Hoover works at Park Royal. He had imported some new machinery from America which he used to make cardboard furniture and he offered to take me on for a pound a week, which was big money in those days. It wasn't so much that I needed a pound a week, but it was the first money I had earned myself, and that was important. Friday was pay day and I can remember that a couple of us would go to the local pub at Park Royal at lunchtime and have a full, four-course meal for three shillings and sixpence. It was our weekly blow-out.'

Chips' sister Joan also remembers him working at Warburton's factory. 'On his first day he made twelve music stands which he was immensely proud of. Then he graduated to candlesticks which were fifteen feet high, and he also made me a rather nice cardboard bedside table, which he later commandeered for his own use.' Chips remembers delivering the candlesticks to Denham Film Studios for the film *I Claudius* when he met the star Charles Laughton.

Chips was made to do all the menial tasks that newcomers get in any factory, sweeping the floors, emptying waste bins and as he says 'shoving the tea trolley around and they weren't slow to tell me if I made a bad mug of tea, friend of the boss or not!'

One of the things Chips learnt right from the start was to be careful not to try to be 'one of the lads'. Even at that age he realised that he needed a certain amount of understanding to get on with people from another, and vastly different, environment. There was one occasion when an initiation ceremony was taking place in the factory. Chips says, 'I crept up to the top floor where this terrific noise was coming from and there stretched out on a table was a young boy, about fourteen years old, stark naked and covered in paper and glue. The other workers were pretending to put a match to him. I wasn't sure what to do but I played it fairly carefully. One had the sense not to try to be one of them.'

It must have been a difficult balance to maintain for a young man recently out of public school. He was living at home in Cadogan Square with the sort of social life he had been used to. His accent immediately placed him apart from his work mates, but at the same time he was expected to mix with them at work and carry out all the dirty tasks he was told to do. As he says now, 'The great leveller of course was our dress. As soon as we got to the factory we changed into dungarees or boiler suits, so we all looked exactly the same.' After a probationary period Chips' wages were boosted to three pounds a week, and that's when he decided to buy his first car. 'It was a beauty, a second-hand two-seater Wolsey Hornet for which I paid £43 and I used to drive her to work every morning, arriving ready for the whistle at eight o'clock and then home again at seven-thirty – they were long hours in those days. But I was shrewd enough not to park it right outside the factory with all the other chaps' bicycles. I used to leave it round the corner.' Chips remained at the factory for a year during which time he lived what he calls a 'Jekyll and Hyde existence'. 'As soon as the final hooter went, I jumped into the Wolsey, drove like mad to get home and hopped straight into the bath before going out for the evening. Sometimes it took a whole hour to get the glue off my fingers.'

A most fashionable hotel in London in the years immediately before the Second World War was the Berkeley. Chips and Joan were frequent visitors and Ambrose and his Orchestra, who were resident there for many years, became one of their favourite dance bands.

By complete contrast, another musical luminary of the day, Sir Adrian Boult, was also a close family friend. The maestro's wife, Anne, had known Chips' Aunt Ethel (of whom more later) for many years and the Boults had stayed at Duart Castle. Many years later, when Chips was in residence, his young daughter Janet asked Sir Adrian for his autograph. He appeared not to hear the request at first. Then a little while later he presented her with a piece of paper on which he had written the first four bars of 'Fingal's Cave' – a rare collectors' item indeed!

Shortly after Chips left the factory he joined the Commonwealth Society and began to take an increasing interest in overseas affairs,

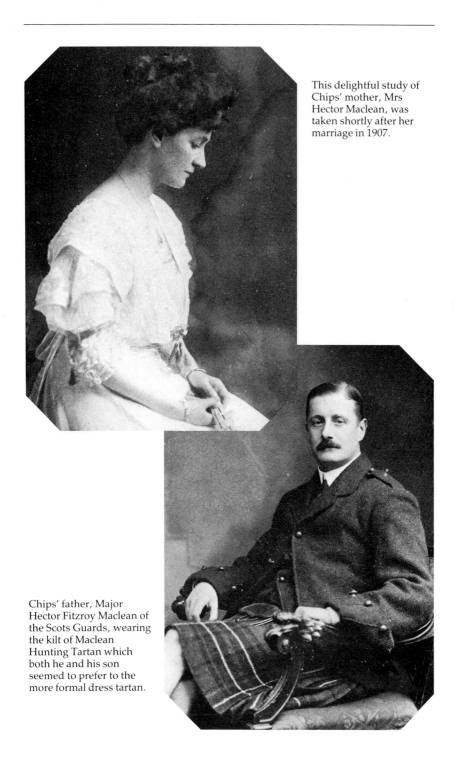

This delightful study of Chips' mother, Mrs Hector Maclean, was taken shortly after her marriage in 1907.

Chips' father, Major Hector Fitzroy Maclean of the Scots Guards, wearing the kilt of Maclean Hunting Tartan which both he and his son seemed to prefer to the more formal dress tartan.

The Chieftains and Pipers
lead the winding
procession of hundreds of
Clansmen from the jetty
towards Duart Castle on
the day 'the Macleans
came home'. The yacht in
the bay belonged to Lord
Llangattock, Sir Fitzroy's
brother-in-law.

'Home coming of the Chief' – Sir Fitzroy Maclean, Bt., 26th Chief of Clan Maclean, being piped ashore at Duart in 1912, accompanied by Lady Maclean, and behind them, Chips' uncle, Captain Charles Maclean, and his mother, Mrs Hector Maclean.

The Macleans gather in front of the partly restored castle for the service of dedication and thanksgiving at the return of Duart to the Clan.

An enthusastic greeting as the Chief is brought to the entrance to Duart: *'Fhir Dhubhairt, tha Clann Illeathain a feitheamh a mach gu cur faillte oirbhann an Luchairt 'ur sionnsaireachd.'* (The Clan Maclean is waiting without to give you welcome in the Castle of your ancestors.)

The largest contingent from overseas came from the USA. Here some of the American Macleans prepare to board the launch at Oban for the short voyage across to Mull.

Major Hector Maclean, home on leave at the end of the First World War, poses in the garden at 9, Gerald Road, London with his three children (left to right) Chips, Donald and Joan.

In the early 1920s family holidays were sometimes taken at Folkestone in Kent where Donald and Chips loved to play on the beach. This is one of Chips' favourite photographs.

Eighty years span the generations – the nine-year-old Chips with his ninety-year-old grandfather, Sir Fitzroy Maclean, the only person who refused to call him anything other than 'Charles'.

'The Emperor's Wife' – a young Chips at Mr Gibbs' Preparatory School in Sloane Street dressed for his part in the school play 'The Emperor's New Clothes'.

By the time he was thirteen, Chips was already starting to look like a young Laird. This photograph was taken on Mull during summer holidays between the two world wars.

something which was to stand him in good stead for the rest of his life, particularly when he became Chief Scout and later Lord Chamberlain. He also joined the Supplementary Reserve, which is the Territorial Army equivalent in the Brigade of Guards. Any young man wishing to take a commission in the Guards before the war without going through Sandhurst was required to belong for a period to the Supplementary Reserve where his potential could be assessed before he was accepted as an officer.

So the pattern his life was shortly to take was beginning to evolve. He was still living at home in central London; there was no immediate need for full-time employment; certainly not on financial grounds and the Army beckoned as the rightful future home of the young baronet. Because by now he had succeeded his grandfather who died in 1936 at the age of 101.

He had also begun to realize what being Chief of a Clan meant and the responsibilities that accompanied the title. He was just twenty when Sir Fitzroy Maclean of Duart died and he says that in fact it was only the year before, at the celebrations to mark his grandfather's one hundredth birthday, that he started to understand what clans and clansmanship were all about.

Hundreds of Macleans from all over the world gathered at Duart Castle on Saturday, 20th May, 1935 to mark the centenary of their Chief. He was a gallant, courteous and generous soldier who had lived most of his life outside Scotland, yet of whom it was said 'the blood is strong and the heart is Highland.'

And so they came to do him honour on his one hundredth birthday. He was too feeble by then to welcome them in person. He remained in his room high in the castle's interior. But his daughter, Mrs Marsham, his younger son, Captain Charles Maclean, and his heir, the youthful Chips, were there to oversee the celebrations which included a cake complete with one hundred candles and a special poem written by the clan Bard, the Rev. Dr Lauchlan Maclean Watt. Four thousand Macleans from all parts of the globe had signed two volumes of an address which was presented to the Chief and the telegram which arrived from Buckingham Palace from King George V exceeded greatly the usual formal greeting which centenarians received. (See page 63.)

This was a fitting tribute from the sailor King to the soldier Chief. The birthday cake was cut by Chips as proxy for his grandfather and it was at that moment that the young Maclean began to realize what it meant to hold 'the honoured Highland name Maclean'.

Just a year later the name was to mean even more to him for in 1936, Sir Fitzroy, who had survived the battles of Alma, Sebastopol and the Charge of the Light Brigade, died peacefully in his sleep, in the place he called home – Duart Castle. Chips can remember the day he died very clearly:

I was having lunch with a school friend of mine named Brayne-Nichols, at his family home in Croydon. As we were sitting down to eat the telephone rang and Mrs Brayne-Nichols went to answer it. She came back, looked at me and said 'Well Chips, I don't know quite what to say. I've got to tell you that your grandfather's died.' I replied that it wasn't unexpected. He was very old and had been under the weather for some time and she then said, 'Yes but what do I call you, Sir Chips or Sir Charles?'

Chips himself, although at the back of his mind had the knowledge that one day he would inherit the title, had never thought of himself as Sir Charles, and on the day following his grandfather's death, he went, accompanied by his sister, to buy a dark suit suitable for mourning, and a black tie, which up to that time he had not possessed:

The shop assistant asked me where to send the clothes and to whom they should be addressed. I said, 'Send them to Mr Maclean at 56, Cadogan Square.' As we left the shop Joan turned to me and said, 'You know you've got to get used to being Sir Charles now.' It was a funny feeling because I hadn't been really brought up to it. I was after all the third man in. It ought to have been my father and after him my brother – it was a strange feeling.

Chapter 3

THE WAR YEARS

Had it not been for the outbreak of the Second World War in 1939, no doubt Chips' life would have revolved around London in the winter and Duart in the summer, with his induction into public life coming as inevitably as the seasons. But it was not to be – at least not for another ten years.

On 21st November, 1936, Chips applied to join the Supplementary Reserve and was granted a commission as a Second Lieutenant in the Scots Guards. In February the following year he was attached to the First Battalion for preliminary training at the Tower of London and for the next two years he attended parades and training camps preparing for what everyone knew was coming sooner or later – war with Germany.

Then on 2nd September, 1939, one day before war was declared, he was called up and posted to the Training Battalion, Scots Guards on mobilization. He was to serve for nearly ten years before he retired as a Major in February, 1949.

The Scots Guards is the regiment of foot guards with the strongest family tradition in the entire guards division. There are many officers and guardsmen who can trace their family associations with the regiment through three and four generations. Chips was following his father, and in turn his son followed him. His daughter married into the regiment and her husband's father and uncle were both Scots Guards.

The regiment was raised in 1642 by King Charles I who ordered the 1st Marquis of Argyll to mobilize 1,500 men to fight in Ireland. This regiment, originally known as Argyll's Regiment, was subsequently renamed the 'Regiment of Scottish Foot Guards' by Charles II, prior to his coronation at Scone on New Year's Day, 1651. It remained under this name until 1712, when Queen Anne decided that the Regiment should henceforth be known as The Third Regiment of Foot Guards. And it was as Third Guards that the Regiment distinguished itself on the battlefields of Dettingen and Waterloo, where its part in the defence of Hougoumont is regarded as one of the epics of that great battle.

More than a hundred years passed before the regiment was renamed yet again. This time by King William IV in 1831, who decided on the title

Scots Fusilier Guards. This was the name under which they fought in the Crimea, where at the battles of Alma and Inkerman they won the Army's first Victoria Crosses. And indeed it was Queen Victoria herself who gave back to the regiment it's original name of Scots Guards in 1877, since when it has distinguished itself in every major campaign from South Africa, through two world wars, to Korea, the Middle East and more recently in Northern Ireland.

The Guards Depot at Pirbright is the first introduction to the rigours of Army life for all those intending to make the Brigade of Guards their future home. In the early years of the Second World War Lieutenant Chips Maclean at the age of twenty-four was responsible for the conduct and discipline of men ten years his senior. Looking back on it he says, 'It was quite extraordinary that they ever did arything I told them to do.'

The Third Battalion was to be joined during the war years by young officers who were to become some of the most distinguished figures in British life. Robert Runcie, now Archbishop of Canterbury, was to win the Military Cross. Willie Whitelaw, a squadron commander, who also won the Military Cross, was to see half his men and tanks destroyed in a single afternoon during the Battle of Caumont shortly after the D-Day landings. He would go on to become one of the most prominent political figures of the post-war years, occupying such great offices of State as Home Secretary and Lord President of the Council. Sir Hector Laing, today one of the world's leading businessmen who heads the international United Biscuit Company, was in the Third Battalion as was 2nd Lieutenant The Earl of Cathcart, who would end the war as a Major decorated with the DSO and the MC. Lord Michael Fitzalan Howard who, thirty years later as Marshal of the Diplomatic Corps, would work in close contact with Chips at St James's Palace, was a regular soldier and commanded Left Flank at the Battle of Caumont, and a very junior Lt M Gow eventually became in 1985 General Sir Michael Gow, the longest serving soldier in the British Army. By any standards a remarkable body of men, with varied talents and, something which was not immediately apparent at the time, a burning ambition to succeed. That so many did succeed, and indeed that so many should simply survive, is a remarkable testament to the quality and tenacity of those war-time recruits. The early years of the Second World War were a strange time for everybody in Britain. Apart from the evacuation of Dunkirk, which was treated as a major victory at the time, for those troops who remained in the United Kingdom it was a lengthy period of consolidation. Training, manoeuvres, drills and more training, with the distant 'second front' a remote and far off target which was not to materialise until 1944.

For Chips and his fellow officers who were stationed near London, the early war years were not unpleasant. Many of the theatres had remained open and the leading restaurants and night clubs did their best to provide entertainment within the limits of strict rationing and the 'blackout'.

Sir Henry Clowes, now retired and living in London, remembers how he and his comrades used to book seats for the Crazy Gang at the Victoria Palace Theatre. The Crazy Gang, Flanagan and Allen, Nervo and Knox, and Naughton and Gold were the country's most popular comedians for more than twenty years and they were particular favourites with members of the Royal Family, especially during the war when their slapstick routines provided hilarious escapism from the realities of the blitz.

Henry Clowes recalls how they used to use Chips' name to get the best seats 'because he had a title and that was one way you could be sure to get in'. After a while the Crazy Gang began to know where the Scots Guards were in the audience and a running joke became one of the hits of the show. Nervo would say to Knox: 'Have you seen anyone special today?' and Knox would reply: 'Yes, I've seen Sir Charles Maclean.' For some reason this would always bring the house down and the name 'Sir Charles Maclean' became one of the catch phrases of the day. Chips himself remembers that he became very friendly with the Crazy Gang after this; going around to their dressing-rooms with his friends to share a drink during or after the show.

Two other members of the Third Battalion in 1940 were the brothers Mann, George and John. They were both famous cricketers who would go on to play for England and the MCC with contemporaries such as Dennis Compton, the Bedser twins and Leonard Hutton. George Mann who went on to become President of the MCC, quickly left the Third Battalion to be posted to the Middle East with the First Battalion where he distinguished himself in action winning the MC and the DSO, but John stayed and became a close friend of Chips. It was to prove the most important friendship of Chips' life because it was through John Mann that he was to meet the girl he would marry.

The summer of 1940 was one of the best on record; the sun shone for hours every day from May until late September and when regimental duties were completed for the day it was possible to relax writing letters home or playing cricket or tennis. And when John Mann invited Chips home for the weekend to play tennis it seemed like a pleasant way of spending a few days so accepted. The Mann family, whose father had played for Middlesex and England, was renowned for its sporting achievements and their house at Ascot was a mecca for everyone who liked to play games. On the first afternoon that Chips arrived he was told by John Mann that he had a chore to perform. His young sister Lizzie was staying at Windsor with friends and he had to go over and drive her home so he invited Chips to go with him for the ride. Chips remembers with extreme clarity his first reaction when he was introduced to Elizabeth: 'I thought, My God, you're absolutely gorgeous.' She was seventeen at the time and had recently started nursing, but Chips made every effort to cultivate the Mann brothers so that he could be invited to their home as often as possible. He even went to the extent of trying to learn something about their lifetime passion – cricket. George Mann told me that one weekend when Chips was there, he had obviously gone to great lengths to try and impress father Mann by introducing cricket into the conversation at every opportunity. He got more and more muddled and finally Mann Senior said with resigned good humour: 'Chips, you are one of the nicest fellows we know but please leave cricket alone – it just isn't worth it.'

John and George Mann had no idea why they had become so popular with Chips. They didn't for an instant think he could be interested in 'our little sister, after all she was just seventeen.' But Chips knew that Elizabeth was the girl for him right from the start and he pursued her with the single-mindedness that has been his guiding light throughout life.

When John and George were finally told of Chips' intentions they were more than slightly startled. As John said, 'Although she was working as a voluntary nurse, to us she was still little more than a schoolgirl.' Chips plucked up courage to ask Elizabeth's father for his daughter's hand and the reply was, 'Well I think you should at least wait until she is eighteen.' Elizabeth was eighteen on a Wednesday in June, 1941. The following Saturday they were married in the Guards Chapel with another officer, Lieutenant Tom (later Sir Thomas) Dundas, as Best Man. As Chips recalled: 'There were lots of wartime romances and marriages which happened at a rapid pace simply because no one knew what was coming next.'

Chips still had the house at 56, Cadogan Square which was to be their home, at least for the time being, but the honeymoon was spent in Scotland at Duart Castle. It was Elizabeth's first visit to the ancestral home and for their honeymoon the State Bedroom had been specially redecorated with the family pooling their wartime clothing coupons so that new coverings could be made for the magnificent four-poster bed.

Elizabeth fell in love with Duart and Mull immediately, which is just as well for she was to spend a major part of the rest of her life living and working on the island. But her short-term future lay as an Army wife and for several years she followed her husband around from camp to camp in various parts of England moving from married quarters to married quarters. Chips says that right from the start Elizabeth was marvellous at making a home from practically nothing. At one time they even spent a week sleeping in the stables at one camp while they were hunting for lodgings.

Even as a young married woman Elizabeth felt very strongly that Duart was her real home and it was important for it to be looked after and lived in, so there were many times when Chips would stay with the Battalion and she would return to Duart, sometimes for months on end. It was a difficult period for many young couples and perhaps even more so for the Macleans with the added responsibility of the upkeep of a castle in a remote part of the Western Highlands. Not only was money required to maintain the structure of Duart, but in wartime Britain it was practically impossible to obtain materials for what was not regarded as essential work.

In the meantime Chips had been promoted to Captain fairly early on in the war. He claims it was not because of any particular merit on his part, simply because he had been in the Supplementary Reserve and had administrative training which meant he knew how to delegate duties. But according to a number of his contemporaries it was not only this that caused him to be promoted. The late Colonel John Harvey:

Chips had an air of quiet authority which made him stand out as someone who could handle responsibility, so I am quite sure that is why he was singled out for early promotion. And another thing is he was respected by the soldiers, which wasn't always the case with officers who were popular.

Early in 1942 a very young, nervous Ensign presented himself in the officers' mess at Codford B Camp on Salisbury Plain. Lieutenant RAK Runcie had come straight from Sandhurst to join the Third Battalion, Scots Guards. Today as The Most Reverend and Right Honourable Lord Archbishop of Canterbury, he resides in Lambeth Palace and ranks behind only the Queen and the Duke of Edinburgh and the Princes of the Blood Royal in order of precedence in England.

Dr Runcie was to distinguish himself as a tank commander winning the Military Cross before the end of hostilities. He remembers his first encounter with Chips who was a Company Commander at this time:

He was a formidable looking figure whose character was extremely difficult to plumb at first. He had this correct, dead-pan, yet puckish mixture which enabled him to play his cards close to his chest and be a very penetrating observer of the human scene. He was as kind as one could be to a new, very junior officer and as we got to know each other better I realised one of the secrets of his success. He was first class at spotting 'originals'. If there was someone who was a bit out of the ordinary Chips could pick this out and he obviously liked people to be a bit different.

His Grace recalls one friendship that at first seemed a strange pairing:

There was a young lieutenant named Harold Llewellyn Smith in Chips' Squadron at the time of the Battle of Caumont. He became the headmaster of a well known grammar school in London after the war. He was a Wykamist and the son of a brilliant man who had been Secretary of Education in Lloyd George's government. He had obtained a First at New College, Oxford, so his academic pedigree was impeccable. But he had devoted a large part of his life to helping underprivileged children from the East End slums, an unusual background for officers in the Brigade of Guards. In the Battalion he was regarded as a formidable brain and his conversation obviously sprang from a well-stocked mind. He had a quiet, sardonic wit and most of us thought of him as the intellectual of the Battalion. But he struck up a close friendship with Chips in spite of the fact that at first they would appear to have had very little in common.

This last refers to the fact that on his own admission Chips has never been regarded as an intellectual; his talents lie in other areas. But Dr Runcie says:

Harold Llewellyn Smith was a very shrewd judge of character and he could tell a phoney at a great distance so he knew there was something in Chips that gave them a common bond.

The Archbishop tells this story as an illustration of how easy it is to underestimate Chips Maclean.

His friendships within the regiment were wide-ranging and covered some of the most unlikely people. There was a young captain, Hugo Charteris, who was to become a best-selling novelist after the war and whose sister married another famous writer, Ian Fleming. Charteris was regarded as the 'Bolshie' of the regiment. He came from an old established Army family with a long and immaculate pedigree, but he was apparently a rebel about Service discipline and tradition; things about which Chips was always absolutely correct. But they became close friends much to the surprise of other officers who thought that Chips, with his attitude to rules and regulations, would be completely at odds with the easy-going and occasionally slapdash Charteris.

The social life of the officers' mess was restrained compared to the pre-war years but Chips was always ready for a party and according to Dr Runcie, the more music the better: 'To see him dance an eightsome reel was elegance itself,' says the Archbishop, 'his deadpan expression completely at odds with his gracious, twinkle toes.'

Chips earned a reputation as the regiment's practical joker and some of the tricks he played on fellow officers, particularly those senior to himself, could have got him into serious trouble. There was one occasion when he decided to promote and post the padre. Apparently this particular cleric was a person Chips didn't exactly hit it off with – in the first place he was a Scottish Presbyterian and Chips is an Episcopalian so they presumably didn't have all that much to do with each other. Anyway as Chips was in charge of Headquàrters Squadron he had access to all sorts of official documents and letterheads. He also had, and still has, an acute eye for detail – his reputation at St James's Palace as Lord Chamberlain was based to a great extent on this facet of his personality – so whenever he perfomed one of his practical jokes, it was always done with great style and was impossible to detect. The padre had been getting on Chips' nerves for some time and finally Chips decided to get rid of him. The padre received an official-looking paper informing him that he had been promoted to Major and that he was being posted with immediate effect to a camp many miles from Salisbury Plain. The padre believed every word of his orders, there was no reason not to, packed his belongings, made his farewells and left for his new station. It was only when he had got half-way that a message was relayed to him, telling him that there had been a mistake and that he had better return to camp. Whether he found out who the perpetrator of the deed was and what transpired between them has never been revealed. If he reads this, it could be the first time that he knows the real story!

On 25th August, 1942, Chips' and Elizabeth's first child was born. Lachlan Hector Charles Maclean, son and heir to the baronetcy and Chiefship of the Clan, came into the world during the high summer of one of the worst years of the Second World War. Within weeks of his birth his parents took him up to Scotland where Jennie Macleod, the long-serving housemaid of the Maclean family, was given the honour of being the first to carry the newest member of the Clan over the threshold at Duart Castle. She remembers it to this day:

Lady Maclean, who looked like the young Judy Garland, was carrying the baby all wrapped up in a white shawl. Just as they were about to enter the castle, Sir Charles (as he then was) said, 'I think Jennie should be the first to carry Lachlan into Duart.' It was a lovely gesture and one I've always treasured.

By now the Macleans had sold their house in central London and bought another at Sunningdale in Berkshire. Elizabeth commuted, when wartime travel restrictions would allow, between this house, wherever Chips happened to be stationed and Duart. The rail and sea journey between Berkshire and Mull in those days could easily take up to twenty-four hours and with a young child in tow it wasn't the pleasantest of trips. Mull was a restricted area at the time with strict security checks on everyone travelling from the mainland. Elizabeth recalls:

We had to carry our identity cards at all times and we also had one or two problems with the 'Blackout' at Duart. But there were compensations; Duart looked out over one of the busiest sea lanes in the world in the 1940s so there was always plenty to see from the battlements as the warships sailed up and down the Sound of Mull as the Atlantic Convoys were being formed.

As the years progressed and D-Day grew closer, the training of the armoured division grew even more intense. Churchill tanks were the vehicles of the Third Battalion and there was a constant round of training and retraining. This was to pay off in the coming months.

As far as Chips and many of his colleagues were concerned the years between 1941 and 1944 were frustrating ones. They saw a lot of their comrades depart for other parts of the world where they were distinguishing themselves in various theatres of war. Prior to the invasion of Normandy Chips' Battalion had been sent to Kent where the rest of the invasion forces were gathering. He remembers being bottled up in Kent for some months while the remainder of the Allied task force was assembled: 'It was a relief when the order to go came at last. We had been waiting about for so long.'

The Third Battalion didn't go over with the first wave on D-Day itself but a couple of weeks later when the beachhead had been established and the landing conditions were suitable to accommodate the Churchill tanks of the 6th Guards Tank Brigade.

Within days of landing on the beach in Normandy the Battalion was in action in a battle that was to provide the bloodiest of introductions to the second front. On 30th July, 1945 they were camped about four miles east of Bayeux and received orders to move with all speed to a concentration area some four miles north of Caumont, a distance of about twenty-three miles. The German army was entrenched in a very strong position and very little was known about the strength of the enemy forces. The countryside around Caumont contained very few roads and the area was covered with cider orchards, so the only vehicles which were likely to be able to move forward over open ground were the Churchill tanks of the Third Battalion. The battle also involved units of the Grenadier Guards, the Argyll and Sutherland

Highlanders, the Seaforth Highlanders, the Gordon Highlanders and the Coldstream Guards.

The battle order of the Third Battalion was: Headquarters Squadron commanded by Major Sir Charles Maclean; Right Flank commanded by Major, The Earl Cathcart; 'S' Squadron commanded by Major W S I Whitelaw and Left Flank under the command of Major The Hon. Michael Fitzalan Howard.

The opposition from the Germans was far greater than expected and the progress towards Caumont was sporadic due to snipers and heavy artillery gunfire. The Churchill tanks were not affected too badly, but the infantry found it difficult to keep up.

Throughout the day the battle raged and eventually, around six in the evening, Major Willie Whitelaw's Squadron tanks were taken by complete surprise when two enormous self-propelled guns emerged from a wood and lumbered up right into the middle of his squadron's position. They were Jagd Panthers, mounting extra long 88-mm guns, the largest machines of their type in existence and never before encountered by the British in action. Their tactics were brilliant and within five minutes no fewer than eleven of the Churchills had been destroyed at point-blank range. Major Whitelaw had lost more than half his squadron on the first day of battle but at least one of the mammoth German guns had been silenced by the tank of Lieutenant David Bankes.

As Major Whitelaw reorganised the remainder of his squadron, Major Sir Charles Maclean arrived with A Echelon to supply fuel and ammunition. The first day of battle for the Third Battalion was over and it was time to count the losses.

Twenty-three officers and men were killed in that one attack; another eighteen wounded. All but four were from 'S' Squadron and the fatalities suffered accounted for one third of the total the Battalion would suffer throughout the campaign in Europe.

The loss of so many Churchill tanks in a single operation was a devastating blow. The Churchill was considered to be the least vulnerable of all British tanks, but no one had considered the impact of the German giant Panther guns. It would have been impossible to do so and never again would the Third Battalion be caught in the same set of circumstances.

On the plus side, the objective had been gained. They had virtually destroyed an entire enemy division and a feeling of mutual confidence between tanks and infantry sprang from that day. Nevertheless, as Chips and his surviving comrades gathered in the darkness of that July evening, they were sadly aware of the large gaps in their ranks.

Willie Whitelaw, now Lord President of the Council and Leader of the

House of Lords, had first met Chips in 1938 when, as a student at Cambridge, he had arrived at Windsor on attachment from the university, to complete his training with the Scots Guards. Chips was then in the Supplementary Reserve and was attending the same training camp. Lord Whitelaw returned to Cambridge, where he was a contemporary of John and George Mann, soon to become brothers-in-law to Chips, and they didn't meet again until 1940 when they were both mobilised. They were to serve together throughout the hostilities in France, Holland and Germany and he was to stand as godfather to Chips' son Lachlan.

Today he recalls that he and his fellow tank commanders were always rather surprised to find Chips, not at the rear where you would expect a Headquarters Commander to be, but up at the front:

We never had to wait for supplies during a battle. You only had to turn around and Chips was there, frequently under fire, with his amazing capacity for unflappability. He appeared to run his squadron without any effort. I'm sure that was not the case because it would have been impossible to do so, but he always made it look easy.

Headquarters Squadron also had responsibility for despatch riders and reconnaisance vehicles. Apparently Chips used to ride alongside his drivers when they were taking their scout cars into enemy territory, knowing that as an officer he would command the respect of his men only if they knew that he was as willing as they were to take the risks.

If he felt any sense of frustration at remaining with Headquarters Squadron while his contemporaries were winning Military Crosses and other decorations for valour as tank commanders, he gave no outward sign. Neither Lord Whitelaw, Dr Runcie, Lord Michael Fitzalan Howard, Lord Elgin, David Bankes or any other of his brother officers ever felt that he resented the role that had been assigned to him, or their success at the 'sharp end' of the armoured division.

As the Battalion moved through Europe they were required to become proficient at coping with the unexpected. They would frequently be ordered to move at a moment's notice – and then find they would be ordered back to their original base at the end of the day. They were stationed temporarily in Eindhoven in Holland when a number of these moves took place. Eventually the inhabitants of the town grew so used to their travels that they became known as the 'Eindhoven Wanderers'.

Major Whitelaw wrote in his diary an account of one such move:

The last alarm was the best. We thought we were going some

distance south. We had looked at the new place and all was set. About 6pm one day we were told that all that move was off. About 1am that night Chips (Major Sir Charles Maclean) and I, were sleeping peacefully when Vernon (Captain V F Erskine Crum) woke us to say we were moving at 8am to an entirely new place some way north. I shot off with the advance party at about 7.30 and the Battalion moved off somehow about 8 . . . Then yesterday, with a little more notice, we were off again, back towards our original place. Now we are sitting here waiting for our next move.

The Battalion forged its way across Europe fighting a number of battles on the way and suffering casualties which further depleted their numbers, but there was nothing to compare with those first day losses at Caumont and most of the action was fought at a distance.

As the Battalion entered Holland they were aware of a slightly more subdued welcome than they had experienced in Normandy and France. This was soon realised to be the aftermath of a rigorous German occupation and the threats of the departing army of what they would do when they returned. The Dutch had experienced the horrors of occupation for too many years to be optimistic about their immediate future and they were wary of showing outward signs of gratitude and hospitality. Within a short time though it became apparent that the Germans were gone for good and the kindness extended to the British troops more than compensated for the initial reservation. In fact Chips remembers that throughout his time in Holland he came across more friendliness to all things British than anywhere else in Europe.

In February, 1945, the Battalion was involved in action at Nijmegen where the main battle was one of supply and communications. The Rhine had flooded and for fifty miles from Nijmegen the roads were covered to a depth of three feet. The official records of the period state:

The Churchills which were still bogged around Kranenburg were now almost submerged, and a water Weasel had to be obtained to rescue valuable stores from them before they eventually disappeared below the water. Until the floods subsided Major Sir Charles Maclean and A Echelon kept the Battalion regularly supplied by DUKW. The Battalion despatch riders did fine work making long, difficult and often dangerous detours through the Reichswald to the South. Undeterred by the shortage of maps and the darkness of the nights, they found their destinations in all hours.

On one occasion Chips was posted 'Missing believed Killed'. He had gone out in one of his jeeps on a scouting mission when they ran into enemy fire. Another vehicle was destroyed and Chips and his driver were lost in the confusion that followed. His brother-in-law, John Mann, was waiting back at Battalion Headquarters when the news came in that Chips had been killed. He says:

I knew that it was going to be up to me to get the news to Elizabeth who was back home with Lachlan who was then just a year old. We were all very depressed, but thankfully before any action had been taken, Chips turned up, as large as life a few hours later. His driver had managed to find his way back through the lines and Chips wondered what all the fuss was about.

As the Battalion sped through Germany Chips was about to come upon the place which was to have such a profound effect on him. As the tanks chased the retreating German army Chips and his Headquarters Squadron arrived at an unknown town by the name of Bergen-Belsen, a name which was to become synonymous with horror. He arrived at Belsen the day after the concentration camp was liberated. They had heard that such places existed but no one had the slightest idea of what they were about to see. Chips says:

We could smell the place miles before we got there but no one could place the smell, it was unlike anything we had come across before. Then as we approached the gates of the camp there were groups of people in these black-and-white pajamas lying around the roads or trying to walk. It was the entrance to a nightmare. I'll never forget the sights that greeted us as long as I live. Piles of bodies all over the place. It was difficult to tell if they were dead or alive. I've never known such a feeling of anger, either in myself or the soldiers. We could not believe that anyone had done such things to other human beings. Piles of corpses were being bulldozed into huge great open pits just as if they were bundles of bricks and the stench was overpowering. The thing I remember most was the wonderful work being done by the doctors and very young nurses who were trying to keep some of the unfortunate people alive.

But the most difficult part of all happened some months later when the Battalion had returned to England. Chips was instructed to lecture to young conscripts on his experiences at Belsen. The memories were still fresh in his mind and he didn't hold back at all. In fact his descriptions of the scenes were a bit too vivid for some of his listeners and one day he was called before a senior officer and told that the lectures had to stop. Chips asked what he was doing wrong and he was told that he was preaching too much hatred of the Germans. He replied that he thought that was what the war had been about and that was what he had been fighting for. The answer was that Britain had been fighting the Nazis not the Germans which he found hard to stomach after what he'd seen at Belsen.

In fact it took Chips some years after the war to get his feelings about the German people into perspective. He says he could never go back to Belsen, but he has a large box of official war photographs taken at the time which he keeps very carefully locked away because he wouldn't like anybody else to see them. He would like to be able to forget what he saw but knows that as long as he lives the memories will remain with him, even if the feelings of anger and disgust towards the Germans have long since mellowed.

The end of the war saw the Third Battalion very near the Russian front at Schleswig-Holstein. Chips says 'We all breathed a sigh of relief that at last it was over – of course for some of us it was just beginning.' This was the famous occasion mentioned earlier when Chips, Robert Runcie and Willie Whitelaw and a number of their colleagues had been celebrating VE Day and the talk turned to prospects for the future.

After several officers had expressed a wish to marry 'rich widows and retire to the Bahamas', the conversation focused on Robert Runcie who had by then decided to enter the church. 'You'll probably end up as Archbishop of Canterbury', the group declared. Then it was Willie Whitelaw's turn. He had shown a leaning towards politics while at Cambridge before the war and they decided he was for the Cabinet. But when the time came to work out a career for Chips, his eye for detail and his administrative genius led them to think of the Royal Household. 'You'll either end up in the Tower of London or working for the Monarch.' The first alternative was because of his reputation as a practical joker. He was the outstanding joker of the regiment and his tricks on his fellow officers carried the true mark of the dedicated hoaxer.

When the Battalion returned to England after the war they learned that if any officer wanted to remain in the Army with a permanent commission he would have to go before the War Office Selection Board, even if he had served with distinction and been decorated for gallantry. The Commanding Officer of the Third Battalion received a complicated form to be filled in by all officers wishing to stay in the Army. It contained a large number of questions which had to be answered by the applicant and also spaces for his suitability to be assessed. Some of the categories were personal in the extreme. Under the heading 'Qualities of Leadership' was a sub-heading 'Sexual Prowess to be marked 1-10.' The Colonel was incensed that his men, members of one of the most exclusive regiments in the British Army, should be subjected to such a humiliating ordeal. He rushed up to London to protest to his superiors, only to be told just before he made a complete fool of himself, that perhaps he should look a litle more closely at the 'official form', which turned out to be the work of one of his Squadron Commanders. Chips had spent hours working on the document which looked completely authentic in every aspect. That was the secret of Chips' success as a practical joker. He went into the most meticulous detail, leaving nothing to chance.

Another of his jokes concerned the misuse of regimental toilet paper. Lord Michael Fitzalan Howard still has a copy of a regimental order instructing all ranks to be economical in the use of toilet paper and warning of dire consequences if the 'wasteful use of same material was discovered'. There were few subjects that were taboo but he did draw the line at one or two 'mess pranks' that threatened to overstep the boundaries of good taste. He refused to allow a wager to take place one evening after dinner, when some of the officers decided to find out how many bottles of claret could be decanted into a contraceptive. The subject was one which Chips felt was not quite right in an officers' mess, and there was no subtlety involved. The essence of his humour has always been the slight debunking of officialdom and always carried out with 'tongue in cheek'.

But he wasn't always the perpetrator, occasionally he was on the receiving end. Like the time he was due to go on leave, driving his Rolls Royce which was his pride and joy. As he left the mess there was quite a gathering of fellow officers to see him off – which was unusual to say the least. He soon found out why. He jumped into the driving seat, put the car in gear – and nothing happened. The rear wheels had been jacked up and were spinning harmlessly. But he took it in good part – and his colleagues knew he could take it as well as dish it out!

With the end of the war, the Household Brigade returned to its ceremonial role as guardians of the Sovereign. Because Chips had joined the regiment at the outbreak of hostilities when all ceremonial duties were suspended for the duration, he had not taken part in any King's Guards until 1946. It was the first time he had worn a bearskin even though he had been in the Guards for seven years. During the Royal Wedding of Princess Elizabeth and Prince Philip, Chips was given a roving commission looking after a group of guardsmen who were lining the route outside Westminster Abbey. During the service itself there was nothing for him to do so he wandered into Dean's Yard where the Glass Coach was waiting to carry the Royal Couple back to Buckingham Palace. He takes up the story:

I've always been a nosey parker and I went over to the coach to have a look inside. The coachman told me that we could hear the service being broadcast from inside the Abbey. He produced a radio set from under one of the seats saying, 'His Royal Highness put it

Top Throughout his time at Canford School in Dorset, Chips was a 'wet-bob' – some of his happiest moments were spent on the river. He also enjoyed rugby, boxing and 'Royal' tennis.

Above, right 'A gentleman always removes his hat when about to kiss a lady' – Chips exchanges traditional greetings with a Maori lady in New Zealand during his Public Schools Empire Tour in 1934. Twenty-five years later they were to meet again when he returned as Chief Scout and she remembered the kiss!

Above, left On the same tour, this time in Australia, Chips poses in time-honoured fashion with a cuddly koala bear. It was in Australia that Chips started his life-long love for the Common-wealth – staying in modest homes in the 'outback' and the Governor-General's residence in Canberra.

Sir Fitzroy Maclean, 10th Baronet and 26th Chief of the Clan Maclean, who, when he was taken to the ruin of Duart as a boy, remarked: 'It is going to be my life's ambition to restore the Castle as a family home and as Headquarters of the Clan.' In 1911, he realised that ambition – at the age of 76!

Chips' sister Joan (now Mrs David Graham-Campbell) walking along the seafront at Margate with Aunt Ethel, a remarkable lady who maintained a fierce independence, even in old age.

'A proud day indeed' – a special greetings telegram from His Majesty, King George V, to one of his most distinguished subjects on the day of his one hundredth birthday, 18th May, 1935. The text far exceeds the usual Royal greeting on such an occasion.

In 1936, Sir Fitzroy Maclean died at Duart. He was 101 years old. Chips and his aunt, Mrs Marsham, lead the mourners as they walk behind his grandfather's coffin from the Castle to his last resting place in the tiny family cemetery, where he was buried facing Duart – in accordance with his final wish.

Elizabeth Mann was seventeen when she became engaged to
Captain Sir Charles Maclean. In this engagement photograph it's
easy to see why Chips' first reaction on seeing her was: 'My God,
you're absolutely gorgeous'.

Elizabeth became a nurse shortly after leaving school, working at a hospital near her home in Berkshire. Here she is in her VAD uniform (Voluntary Aid Detachment).

A wartime wedding – just a week after Elizabeth's 18th birthday. They were married in the Guards Chapel with a military Guard of Honour provided by the Scots Guards and the Battalion Piper was on hand to make sure they got off to a musical start!

During the push across Europe shortly after D-Day, you did the best you could in the matter of personal hygiene! Even in an armoured division, the old military adage about 'an army marching on its feet' is observed. This is Normandy, 1944.

Chips with a group of his contemporaries in the Mess of Third Battalion Scots Guards in Germany during the war. Chips is resting on one of the Regimental trophies – the officer sitting next to him (and looking slightly sceptical) is Lt. R.A.K. Runcie (now Archbishop of Canterbury).

Willie Whitelaw and Chips giving their ladies a helping hand as they set off on a 'friendly' bicycle race just after the war.

The heir to the Chiefship on his first public occasion. Chips' and Elizabeth's son, Lachlan, at his christening at Windsor. The group includes Miss Peggy Mann, Miss Barbara Chrichton, Lachlan's godfather, Capt. William (now Viscount) Whitelaw and Chips' sister Joan (Mrs David Graham-Campbell).

In 1949 Chips and Elizabeth went to South Africa to watch her brother George Mann play cricket for England in the Test Series. Here Elizabeth is boarding a DC3 at East London for the flight to Cape Town.

Chips has forgotton how many cars he has owned, but this one, a Jaguar SS100 of the pre-war era, was certainly one of his favourites. He started with a two-seater Wolsely Hornet which he bought for £43 and graduated to a Rolls Royce when he was in the Army.

here so they could hear the commentary on the way back up The Mall.' I was also shown the lights that had been installed inside the coach so that onlookers could see Princess Elizabeth and her husband on this dull, dark November afternoon. It was a rather primitive affair with great bundles of batteries stored under the seats.

It was the first Royal occasion that Chips was to attend, little realising that more than twenty years later he would spend a great deal of his time supervising such events.

Most of Chips' colleagues had decided what they wanted to do with their lives. Some had left the Army and were pursuing careers in civilian life. He realised that he had gone as far as he was likely to in the immediate future, and his thoughts began to turn to an alternative lifestyle. Some of his wartime contemporaries think he was wrong in assuming that he had come to the end of the road in the regiment and perhaps he could have gone on to command if he had remained. This is borne out by the fact that he did act as Commandant of the Guards Depot at Caterham for several months, which was a tremendous thrill to him, but he had decided that the responsibilities of Duart and his family outweighed the opportunities in the Army, and he resigned his commission on 2nd February, 1949.

Like most soldiers he is modest about his achievements. But on 22 March, 1945 he received a Mention in Despatches. The citation reads:

Major Sir Charles Maclean Commanded HQ Squadron of the 3rd Tank Battalion throughout the campaign from Normandy to the end of the war. In this capacity it was his duty to bring up the supplies to the tanks from A Echelon. He always came up personally with the Transport and never failed to deliver all that was required in every situation. Even when flooding necessitated the use of amphibious transport, supplies were delivered by him as regularly as usual. His organising ability and his skillful and energetic leadership contributed very largely to the maintenance of the fighting efficiency of the Battalion.

So after ten years in the Scots Guards, Chips returned to Duart to assume responsibility for the castle and clan and to take up his new role as a farmer and landowner. He would have been content to retire from all other duties and live quietly as a country gentleman; but it was not to be. Indeed, the most exciting years of his life were still to come.

Chapter 4

THE FAMILY

When Chips' grandfather, Sir Fitzroy, died in 1936, he left his grandson not only his title and baronetcy, but also a substantial fortune. It meant that for the first time in his life the new Sir Charles Maclean was financially independent; able to do anything he wanted within reason, and also, and much more important from his point of view, help those members of his family who might not always have the means to help themselves.

One in particular came in for a certain amount of assistance and that was Aunt Ethel, his mother's only sister. After Chips inherited he was able to help her occasionally and repay some of the many kindnesses this very special aunt had bestowed on him from an early age. It might be helpful at this point to look at both sides of Chips' family tree.

His paternal grandfather Sir Fitzroy Maclean had married Constance Ackers who was the younger daughter of George Holland Ackers, a member of the landed gentry who lived at Morton Hall in Cheshire. Constance and her elder sister were the heirs to a considerable fortune and it was with her assistance that the London house at 15, Hyde Park Terrace was bought, but it was through an inheritance from Emily, one of Sir Fitzroy's own four sisters, that he was able to buy back Duart Castle in 1911, and mount the extensive restoration programme that was necessary before it became habitable once again.

Chips' maternal grandparents were named Wilding and Williams. His grandfather John Hoskins Wilding was a clerk who worked for his father who owned a small quarry in the Welsh border county of Shropshire. In the matriculation papers published when Chips became a baronet, it was mistakenly stated that his maternal grandfather was 'a clerk in holy orders'. It should have said 'a clerk'. He married a Miss Williams, the daughter of a doctor living at Worksop in Nottinghamshire. Grandfather Wilding was killed in an explosion at the quarry in 1872, leaving his young widow with one daughter and expecting another child, who turned out to be Chips' mother, Winifred.

To be left a widow without independent means, was a fearsome fate in the 19th century, but Mrs Wilding was no ordinary woman, and she soon set about securing a future for herself and her two daughters. She managed to get a job in Yorkshire as governess to the children of a well known family named Pallines. The salary was £100 a year with the added bonus of a cottage that went with the job. In addition Mrs Wilding was allowed to include her own children in the lessons she gave and from these early beginnings she instilled in them a love of letters that was to last them throughout their lives.

A few years after moving to Yorkshire she again demonstrated her remarkable talents as an independent spirit when she founded a girls school in Surrey. She chose the area because it was close to the Royal Military Academy at Sandhurst, and in those days officers did not take their young children abroad with them, but left them in the comparative safety and comfort of home. Mrs Wilding realised there was a need for a school for the daughters of officers and, even though she possessed no formal qualifications, the school was an immediate success and both it and she prospered. Chips' grandmother even found time to write a number of short stories, some of which were published, so obviously this is where he got his literary talents, which were to result in his own children's book a few years ago.

The elder daughter, Chips' Aunt Ethel, also inherited her mother's artistic talents. She was a keen gardener, enthusiastic painter and a more than competent wood-carver. She had a gift for languages and spoke French fluently. Ethel married a Scot, James McArthur from the Highlands, but there were no children and shortly after they were married he left to work in the Canary Islands where he caught a fever and died. So she too, like her mother before her, was left a widow after an all too short marriage. It was during the years of the First World War that she distinguished herself in an unusual way. She volunteered to work in the munitions factory at Woolwich Arsenal where the girls suffered the extremely unpleasant effects of spending hours in an atmosphere which gradually turned their skin yellow – through the presence of the chemicals used in the process of making shells and bullets. Ethel decided to capture the scenes for posterity and she spent many hours sketching the girls at work, the results of which are contained in a large book of drawings which is still in the family.

This then was the lady Chips was able to help. Not that she had ever asked for any help, or indeed welcomed it when it was offered. Even in old age Ethel remained as fiercely independent as ever and the circumstances in which she lived were chosen because that was exactly the way she wanted to live.

So Chips at the age of twenty became Sir Charles Maclean Bt, head of the family and Chief of the Clan Maclean. He was also acutely aware that he was now responsible for the upkeep of Duart Castle and his presence would be required in Scotland with much more regularity than it had been until that time. As he says, 'It was a worry. I knew I had charge of this ancient home and all the responsibilities that went with it including the clan about which I knew very little.'

Nevertheless, the responsibility was accepted and borne with grace by the young baronet. Jeannie Maclean remembers the first time he came to Duart as the new Chief. 'I had grown up with him and knew him as Chips all my life. Now here he was, Sir Charles Maclean, head of the Clan and the most important man on the Island. It was the most natural thing in the world to call him Sir Charles – and much later His Lordship. It didn't alter our relationship as far as I was concerned. He remained one of my oldest and best friends, but he was the Chief. There was no mistaking that and I wouldn't have it any other way.'

Basically he hasn't altered a great deal since those days even though now he is titular head of a very large family as Chief of the Clan, his own immediate family is a close-knit, tight community whose privacy is jealously guarded. His closest companion is still his wife Elizabeth as she has been for the past forty-five years and he is the first to acknowledge her as his best friend and life-long supporter.

At the tender age of eighteen she was introduced into the rigours of life in a remote Scottish castle – and then left to get on with it; even bringing up two children mostly on her own because their father was away soldiering at first and then travelling the world as Chief Scout.

Chips' son Lachlan recalls those early years:

For most of my youth my sister Janet and I learned to lean fairly heavily on Mother, who in many ways, has always been the stronger half of the partnership.

Elizabeth comments:

It's just that I was around a little more than Chips, so perhaps the children, quite naturally, remember me as the ever-present parent, when in fact for most of the time he was abroad they were also away at school.

It is a fact that Elizabeth has spent more time at Duart than Chips. She was left for months on end having to cope with draughty rooms, temperamental plumbing and leaking roofs during the wet and dismal winters that characterise that part of the Western Isles.

But she is not one to complain and she has little patience with anyone who 'whines'. She can hardly have known what she was letting herself in for when she took on the role of mistress of Duart when she was barely out of school, but she has grown to love the castle and the people who live on Mull, as much as she would have had they been her own birthright. As she claims today: 'In some ways I'm more Scottish than any of them.'

In most families there is usually a special relationship between a father and his daughter. Janet has always regarded Chips as a romantic figure who would arrive at Duart from a distant part of the world and was always dashing off to some exotic-sounding place like Zanzibar or Fiji. And when he took her with him on a trip to Australia she was able at first hand to observe the near adulation of the tens of thousands of Scouts and Cubs to whom the Chief was a legendary and heroic figure. She saw him striding around the lines of tents in his kilt and snakeskin belt and then leading his followers in rousing singsongs around a flickering camp-fire. So perhaps it's not altogether too surprising that her view of her father might appear to an outsider to be slightly biased.

Janet is now the Hon. Mrs Barne and she and her husband, a former Major in the Scots Guards, live in a delightful manor house just outside Norwich where he grows strawberries and from where she runs a successful florists business. There are two children, both with good old Scottish names – Alistair and Hamish. One of Janet's fondest memories of her father was when she was at school in London and he would take her out for an evening meal: 'Complete with wine, grown-up talk and the occasional dance.' He treated her as an adult during those impressionable formative years, which is of course exactly the way every teenage girl wants to be treated.

When Chips was appointed Lord Chamberlain, Janet moved back with the family to live in St James's Palace, an experience she enjoyed tremendously. And when she was married in the Guards Chapel, the wedding reception was held in the State Rooms in the palace; a privilege granted by the Queen to only a few of her subjects.

So there were obviously great compensations in having a parent who was close to the greatest in the land. Not many fathers can send their daughters off in such splendid and unique fashion!

While Lachlan Maclean remembers Duart as being 'spooky and very cold', his sister looks back on her childhood as a time of enchantment. The long corridors were ideal for roller-skating and, because there was no television in those days, the family used to join in playing games like Monopoly and Scrabble. Until she was eight years old Janet was educated at home by a succession of governesses. 'There were rather a lot,' she admits. 'They didn't seem to stay very long, perhaps because of the bleakness of Duart or maybe I was to blame – anyway they seemed to come and go with remarkable regularity.'

When she was eight Janet was sent to board at a preparatory school in Perthshire which she quite enjoyed because 'being still North of the Border, it wasn't like being away from home.' It was while she was at school that she first became aware that to be the daughter of the Chief of the Clan was something special, though at first she couldn't understand the interest of the other girls when she gave her address as Duart Castle.

It was also around this time that Miss Janet – as she was known on Mull – began to take on her first public engagements. She remembers being taken to the pier at Craignure and cutting a ribbon to open a 'hut'. But apart from these odd occasions she was treated in the same way as all the other children in the village, wearing plimsolls in the summer and Wellingtons in the winter – shoes were strictly reserved for school and family outings!

Lachlan Maclean had been entered for Eton on the day of his birth, following the tradition set by his grandfather and now to be continued by his own son Malcolm. Because of the great distance between school in Berkshire and home in Scotland he spent many of his half-term holidays with his maternal grandparents at their home in Wiltshire. Then when he left Eton the question of his future was more or less left to him to decide. As he put it: 'There wasn't a great deal of career counselling in the Maclean family.' So he decided to continue the family tradition and join the Scots Guards.

His choice proved to be the right one and his military career was distinguished and colourful, including three and a half years with the SAS about which he will say nothing and the Regiment's Headquarters are equally reticent.

Lachlan is married to Mary, the daughter of a wealthy Scottish farmer and they live in Perthshire with their four children. At the age of twenty-nine, having reached the rank of Major, Lachlan retired from the Army because as he said: 'It was a case of staying in for life, which I didn't particularly want to do, or leaving before I was thirty, which would give me a chance to start a new career.'

He received a number of offers and accepted a job with United Biscuits, the giant food conglomerate which is headed by Sir Hector Laing, one of Lord Maclean's wartime comrades in the Third Battalion, and on the board of which John Mann, Elizabeth's brother, sits as a non-executive director.

Lachlan is honest enough to admit that there was a touch of nepotism in getting his initial interviews, but after that 'I was on my own.'

He now works from the company's headquarters in London but still has his home in Scotland. He freely admits that the main reason he is working is to save Duart. He is not going to inherit a large fortune and he passionately wants to be able to keep Duart. In fact he probably has a closer feeling for the castle than his father. His early years were spent there and he has known all his life that he will one day inherit the Chiefship of the Clan and all its responsibilities. It's something he will welcome when the time comes and he is already trying to make financial arrangements so that he will not take on a financial millstone, which is what Duart has become in recent years.

The Hon. Lachlan Maclean is Adjutant of the Queen's Bodyguard in Scotland, the Royal Company of Archers, of which his father is a Lieutenant. Father is rarely active in the Bodyguard these days mainly, he says, 'because my uniform has been cannibalised to provide Lachlan's with enough gold braid.'

And Lachlan's son, Malcolm, became the third generation of Macleans to enter Royal service in November, 1985, when he was appointed a Page of Honour and attended the Queen at the State Opening of Parliament.

As a family the Macleans are an easy-going and informal group who remain in fairly close contact with each other. Lady Maclean is a vivid personality with tremendous energy and a fierce love of family and home. Both she and the children take great pride in the achievements of Chips – though they would never say so to his face.

Perhaps the strongest characteristic of all about this family is its sense of unity. If any of them is in need of help, it is to each other that they turn and when one of them achieves something, they all celebrate. Chips takes a deep pride in his son's distinction as a soldier and when Lady Maclean needed a Senior Lady-in-Waiting to attend her at the Palace of Holyroodhouse during Chips' time as Lord High Commissioner, it was natural for her to ask Janet – and equally natural for Janet to accept.

They all think that Chips does too much for someone who is supposed to be retired, and secretly he's delighted at their concern.

Chapter 5

DUART CASTLE

Duart Castle has been the spiritual, if not the physical, home of the Clan Maclean for more than 700 years. It first appeared on record in 1390 when it was no more than the original square Keep, built of granite and built on granite, rising out of the rocky shore itself, to dominate the sea approaches from Oban, and the inhospitable land approaches across the peat bog behind it. Yet the foundations of the castle are believed to be even older; probably 1250 was the starting date for the earliest excavations.

The site was chosen for its strategic importance as a fortress against invaders, and the success of that choice has been demonstrated many times over the centuries, in that Duart is one of the few castles remaining in Scotland which has never in its entire history fallen to the force of arms. 'Not altogether surprising', says the present Chief of the Mac-leans. 'My ancestors built the walls more than twelve feet thick at a time when the worst bombardment they could expect was from bows and arrows.'

On the more vulnerable landward side the walls are thirty feet high and a deep ditch was cut through solid rock beyond the walls as an outer defence-work. On the seaward side the only access was a steep, precipitous stone staircase, built of such narrow design that it is barely possible for two men to pass each other, so obviating the possibility of a mass attack.

Duart is situated on a high crag at the end of a peninsula (its name *Dubh Ard* is Gaelic and means 'Black Point') and juts out into the Sound of Mull from where it commands the channel between Mull and the mainland, the entrances of Lock Linnhe and Etive, and the neck of the Firth of Lorne as it meets the Sound of Mull.

The ferry from Oban docks at Craignure after passing directly below the castle walls. As you approach Mull, the landscape is fairly feature-less at first, then suddenly the isolated majesty of Duart rears out of the gloom and it's easy to imagine the daunting sight it must have appeared to would-be invaders in the 15th and 16th centuries.

Duart is one of eight castles built within sight of each other along both sides of the Sound of Mull, which were utilised by the Lord of the Isles as a defensive alliance. A unique signalling system was used by which beacons lighted at Mingary Castle on Ardnamurchan Point, could be seen and repeated the length of the Sound as far as Dunollie Castle near Oban on the Firth of Lorne. Dunollie is another castle which has remained in the same family since it was built. The present owner is Madame Macdougal of Macdougal, a life-time friend and distant neighbour of Lord Maclean.

The man responsible for the building of the original Keep at Duart and founder of the Maclean dynasty was Gillean of the Battleaxe, a maurauding, war-like ruffian who hunted animals and enemies alike with the same implacable ruthlessness and skill. Like all good Scottish castles Duart has its legends. One of which concerns the treasure lying many fathoms deep in Tobermory Bay, but this is a 'legend' based on fact. In 1588 the remnants of the Spanish Armada were scattered all around the coast of Britain by terrible storms and a great Spanish galleon, the *Florencia*, said to contain many chests of gold and silver coins, had taken shelter in the bay. The crew of the galleon needed provisions and they were given permission to hunt for game on Mull, provided their soldiers assisted the then Chief of the Clan, Lachlan Mor Maclean, in his feud with the Macdonalds. The feud had begun over the right to control the sea routes from Argyll to Ulster, a very profitable business, and one which resulted in a great deal of bloodshed for more than ten years as the warring clans battled over who should have control.

The Spaniards agreed to the bargain, and a number of highly trained and armed soldiers joined the Macleans in an expedition against the Macdonalds. But the foray was destined to fail, and Lachlan, seeking to gain something from the ill-fated expedition, seized some of the soldiers, who were then locked in chains in the dungeons of Duart, while the Chief's son, Donald Glas, was sent to the ship to demand payment for their release, and for the food they had taken. Once on board the Spanish galleon, Donald realised that he too was now a hostage and that the ship was preparing to sail. Fearing the attentions of the Inquisition more than death itself, he asked to be allowed on deck for a final farewell look at his homeland. While he was on deck he managed to find a powder magazine and blow up the ship with himself and all the Spanish treasure on board.

The *Florencia* sank within minutes and its wreck still lies on the seabed in Tobermory Bay. The right to recover the wreck and its treasures was granted to the Duke of Argyll by Charles I, and since that time there have been countless attempts by the family to reach it, all to no avail. Legend has it that the *Florencia* was a paymaster ship laden with doubloons, but so far the treasure, which would be worth millions today, has remained in its watery safe. There is no doubt that the ship existed and indeed its whereabouts have been pinpointed fairly accurately. And the present Duke of Argyll takes the matter seriously enough to have mounted a number of diving expeditions to see if the treasure is still there, but the finds to date have been mainly domestic items which would be found on board almost any ship of the period. A small cannon was recovered some time ago and it now rests, appropriately, in the Sea Room of Duart Castle.

Sir Lachlan Maclean was to live for another ten years after the explosion on board the *Florencia* before he was killed on Islay in a battle with the Macdonalds. During his lifetime he had even enlisted the help of Elizabeth I in his war against the Macdonalds and this ultimately proved the downfall of the Clan and the destruction of Duart. Both the Macleans and the Macdonalds had been weakened by the years of interclan warfare and the deaths of their Chiefs, and the mighty Campbells, who were influential in the Stuart Court, were quick to seize the opportunities of capitalising on their misfortunes. The Campbells informed James VI of Lachlan's involvement with Elizabeth I and the King was swift to show his disapproval. He agreed to the sequestration of Duart in 1604 to the King's Commissioners. In 1608 Lord Ochiltree was dispatched to Mull as Viceroy in an attempt to subdue the fighting Chiefs of the Islands. He anchored his flagship near Aros Castle about ten miles from Duart and one of the first things he did was to invite all the Chiefs to join him for a meal on board the ship. In the diplomacy of the day, his Lordship proposed the loyal toast and then informed his guests that they were under arrest. They were transported to Edinburgh in chains, where under duress, they were forced to sign the Statute of Iona, under which they lost effective sovereignty over the islands they had ruled.

As a gesture, the Macleans were permitted to retain Duart Castle but they lost control over much of the lands they had previously owned. So denied their normal pursuits, the Macleans set about a period of domestic consolidation during which the castle was greatly enlarged, and made a much more comfortable home for the Chief and his family.

The first era of Duart had come to a close and the 'old part' dating from 1250 was to be improved by the addition of the 'new part' which was added in 1631. These days, visitors to Duart are intrigued when they are told that the 'new part' of the castle dates from the early 17th century. The inner doorway at Duart has the date 1633 inscribed on it together with the initials SLM, Sir Lachlan Maclean.

If Sir Lachlan had had his warlike tendencies curbed by the Treaty of Iona, the Macleans nevertheless remained soldiers which is what they had always been and which they would continue to be, right up to the present day. And in spite of their treatment by James VI, the Clan remained loyal to the monarchy and this loyalty was rewarded when

Charles I conferred the baronetcy on Sir John Maclean. In 1651 Sir Hector Ruadh Maclean was killed at Inverkeithing in a battle with the Roundheads in which 500 Maclean clansmen died, including it is said, eight of his foster brothers.

But it was the same loyalty to the Stuart cause that would be the end of Duart as the family seat for another 200 years. A large part of the estates around Duart had been mortgaged in order to raise funds to fight for the King. The Campbells, who had been unable to win the territory by conquest, bought up the debts, and eventually they owned most of the Maclean lands. Duart itself remained in Maclean hands in spite of repeated attempts by their traditional enemies to gain control. But eventually Duart was sequestered and handed over to the Campbells after the Battle of Killiecrankie in 1689, when Sir John fought on the losing side. He went into exile and began the long tradition of Maclean Chiefs who were to live outside Scotland. Sir John returned briefly in the ill-fated rebellion of 1715, when again he was on the losing side at Sheriffmuir. He retired abroad once more, where he died a year later, a broken man.

By 1745 the Maclean estates had been forfeited with a seige, and bombardment by English warships, and the defeat of the Jacobites enabled the Campbells to return to Duart with a force of more than 2,500 men who were able to capture the castle and lay it waste. The destruction of Duart was not only an act of vandalism by the victorious Campbells; it symbolised the end of the rebellion as far as the Highlands was concerned. The roof was torn off and the living quarters left open to the elements. It was the beginning of a long period of desolation in the history of Duart, because even though for six years after the '45, English troops were garrisoned in the castle; no restoration or repair work was carried out, and when the soldiers finally left in 1751, Duart was left to stand alone and dilapidated as a stark reminder of days long gone.

The Macleans were scattered all over the world, some deported after the failure of the '45 Rebellion; others travelled throughout Britain and abroad seeking the living which was denied them in their homeland. The new owners of Duart neglected it and despised it. Now that they had it, they no longer wanted it. They simply wanted to prevent the Macleans from occupying it ever again, and in this their task was made easy by the fact that no Maclean would be able to afford to buy back the castle for nearly 200 years.

Many visitors came to Mull in the intervening years and most of them were intrigued by the deserted, mysterious ruin they saw only from the sea. Dr Samuel Johnson and his friend, the diarist James Boswell, visited Mull during their Hebridian tour, when they were entertained by Sir

Allan Maclean, who lived on the nearby islet of Inchkenneth with his three daughters. Sir Allan was another soldier who had come home. Not to Duart which was beyond his means, but as near as he could get. According to Boswell's account of the visit, Johnson found great favour with Sir Allan, even going so far as to wear a broadsword and shield on one occasion, as a tribute to the Highlanders. As they sailed from Inchkenneth on their journey back to Oban, they passed beneath the gloomy ruins of Duart, shrouded in mist and legend.

And then came the man who was responsible for restoring the pride of the Maclean Clan and giving them back their spiritual home. He was born in 1835. Sir Fitzroy Maclean was the 10th Baronet and 26th Chief of the Clan. He was also one of the most romantic figures in recent Scottish history and a man who had but one aim throughout his life: to buy back and restore to it's former glory, the home of the Maclean Clan – Duart Castle.

Like so many of the Highland Chiefs he was born outside Scotland and lived for most of his life beyond it's borders. But there was never the slightest doubt in his mind or his heart that he was a Scot, a Highlander and a Maclean.

In his early youth just a few years after Queen Victoria came to the Throne, Fitzroy was taken to Mull by his father, on leave from Malta, where he commanded the garrison. The young Fitzroy made a vow there and then that one day he would return and take possession of his birthright, in the name of the Macleans throughout the world. He was to keep his word, though it would taken him very nearly the rest of his life. He never forgot what he had promised to do and in 1908, when one of his four sisters, Emily, died, she left him £63,000 in the hope that this might be used towards the restoration of Duart. He journeyed to Mull where he sought out the widow of Murray Guthrie who lived next door to the ruin of Duart, and whose family had owned it since the middle of the 19th century. Mrs Guthrie realised the importance of Duart to Sir Fitzroy, who was seventy-six years old by this time, and agreed to sell the ruined castle and one hundred acres of ground. Sir Fitzroy finally took possession in 1911.

So after nearly 200 years of wandering the world, the Macleans at last had their rightful home restored to them. But all Sir Fitzroy Maclean had bought was an empty, roofless shell. Sheep had roamed freely through its rooms and towers for more than a century, and the castle itself was completely uninhabitable in its present state. It required a massive injection of money to bring the old place back to life and Fitzroy Maclean was determined to see that it was done. Sir John Burnett, a noted architect of the day, based in Edinburgh, was commissioned to draw up plans for the restoration. The walls of the castle were still in magnificient condition because, of course, granite does not deteriorate; they were as solid at the beginning of the 20th century as they had been 700 years earlier. But apart from the walls there was nothing. Burnett had the use of the plans which had been drawn up by the Board of Ordnance in 1748 when the castle was used by the English garrison, and it was from these that he worked to rebuild Duart as it had been.

The main problem was the roof. To make sure that it would withstand the gales which sweep that part of the Western Isles for many months of the year, massive slates from the quarries of Caithness were used, some of them weighing more than 60 lbs each. There was plenty of skilled labour available and masons, carpenters, cabinet-makers and plumbers were imported from nearby Oban to complete the work. The original outside narrow staircase on the seaward side of the castle was still intact, but the architect decided, with Sir Fitzroy's agreement, to enclose the staircase to make it more comfortable and safe to use all year around. This he did by the simple expedient of building an extension to the shoreside wall which encompassed the staircase. The extension, which is known as the Sea Room, is a truly splendid addition to the castle, containing an enormous picture window, from which, on clear days, it is possible to see the peak of Ben Nevis, thirty miles away.

The original front door of the Keep leads into the Banqueting Hall in the very heart of the castle. In its original state the Hall was a long narrow room, bereft of any charm and totally unsuited to modern living, so Sir John changed its aspect by cutting an extension through the twelve-foot thick rear wall, making the room L-shaped, and installing a large window in the L section. This turned a somewhat featureless room into an elegant and gracious apartment which contains pictures of Macleans past and present, as well as a collection of Highland finery with 16th-century documents, 18th-century pistols, swords, silver trinkets, medals and a number of elegant ceremonial dirks and brooches, owned by various members of the family. The Banqueting Hall has managed to achieve that rare compromise between ancient splendour and modern-day comfort, without losing any of its original atmosphere and character. The fireplace incorporates the Coat of Arms of the present Chief, Lord Maclean, and suspended over it are three banners in silk. They are the Regimental Colours of the 236th Battalion, Canadian Expeditionary Force, the Maclean Kilties of America (Sir Sam's Own). The Stars and Stripes were presented by Col. Walter Scott, New York Scottish; the French Tri-colour was presented by His Honour, Mayor James M Curley of Boston, Mass; and, the Union Flag was presented by

Mrs Lewis Nixon of New York. The regiment itself was raised in 1917 by Lt Col Percy A Guthrie (whose mother was born a Maclean), and it was the last regiment to be raised in Canada under the voluntary system. The regiment wore the kilt of Maclean Hunting Tartan throughout the First World War and were recruited from every Province in Canada and twenty-one American States. On the day they embarked from Canada for France they were 1,084 strong. The colours were handed over to Duart and will remain at the castle as long as Duart remains in the possession of the Chief.

The ceiling of the Banqueting Hall is of Norwegian pine, fashioned into enormous rafters which in turn form the floor of the rooms above. To get into the upper part of the castle from the Banqueting Hall one has to climb a complicated spiral staircase which was built inside the thickness of the wall of the Keep. It was ingeniously spiralled clockwise to allow defenders to wield their swords in their right hands.

Originally the upper floor was one giant chamber where the clansmen who lived in the castle would sleep together, rolled in their kilts, ready to repel any attackers. Sir John Burnett divided the available space into the State Bedroom and Dressing Room. The State Bedroom is beautifully decorated with a sturdy four-poster bed whose covers were specially designed and made for the return of Lord Maclean and his young wife on their honeymoon in 1941. The room also contains a handsome writing bureau which once belonged to William Wordsworth. The Dressing Room, or Ante Room as it's known, is also used to house a small display of military uniforms, and the furniture shows some of the strong French influence which was apparent in the Highlands in the 18th century.

On the top floor of the castle a suite of rooms has been coverted into a gallery containing an exhibition devoted to Scouting and on view are many of the souvenirs presented to Lord Maclean during his thirteen years as Chief Scout. From this floor one is able to go out on the ramparts from where, on clear days, the view is truly magnificent, and from where it is possible to see just why Lachlan the Battleaxe chose the site in the first place. The castle dominates the surrounding territory, on land and sea, for more than thirty miles. It's easy to see why no Maclean is recorded has having been killed in battle on his home ground of Duart.

It was Sir Fitzroy Maclean's dream and he lived to see it fully realised. On 12th August, 1912 after a lifetime spent in the service of his country, this soldier, scholar and builder had returned to the Highlands to reclaim his natural inheritance. There was a huge gathering of the Clan at Duart on that August morning as Sir Fitzroy Maclean once more hoisted the Maclean standard above the ramparts as a signal to the world that the Macleans had come home.

There was still a great deal of work to be done before the castle was finally restored to Sir Fitzroy's satisfaction; in fact it was another four years before he took up residence permanently. In that time he also acquired a further thousand acres of land, to supplement the hundred he had bought originally, and gradually he began spending more and more time in Duart, and less in his London home at Hyde Park Terrace. When Sir Fitzroy died in 1936 at the age of 102, he died as he would have wished; peacefully in his own bed looking out across the Sound of Mull 'a true Highlander'.

Duart was to provide a home for Lady Maclean and her two small children for part of the war years, and then in 1949, when Lord Maclean left the Army after his war service, he took up residence once more. At that time the family lived in the whole of the castle, as Chips remembers with a certain amount of ironic nostalgia, 'carrying an oil stove around with as we moved from room to room.' It may seem a romantic place to live from a visitor's viewpoint, but rooms with 14th-century walls twelve feet thick are not the easiest places to heat.

In 1951 a young captain in the Royal Navy, David Mellis, brought his training frigate into the Sound of Mull on an exercise. He and some of his crew were invited to visit Duart Castle – and David Mellis has been on Mull ever since his retirement.

A few years later he left the navy and came to live in the cottage in Aros he had bought shortly after meeting Lord Maclean for the first time. Chips by now had realised that Duart was not a practical proposition even as a summer home and he decided that the only way to keep the castle going was to open it to the public.

David Mellis was enlisted as the 'Clerk of Works' to oversee the alterations that were needed before the public could be admitted. As he recalls:

The castle was impossible to keep warm. Sir Fitzroy had installed central heating in the renovations of 1911, and it was a full-time job for one man to keep the boilers stoked. A small steamer known as a 'puffer' used to dump one hundred tons of coal on the beach just below the castle and the locals would help unload it before it was manhandled up to the cellars of the castle. When I came into the act Chips used to lend a hand.

David Mellis had been given a short but explicit brief:

I was told that we wanted the public to be able to come into the castle at one end, see all the State Rooms and Public Apartments and then leave at the other end of the castle, without impinging too much on the privacy of the family.

This was achieved by moving the family into the East Wing, in an entirely self-contained set of rooms. They are extremely comfortable and much more easily managed than the main rooms. For example, visitors today will see the kitchen which was built into the thickest part of one of the lower walls in 1911. The cooking range and the large pots and pans were those in use at the time and, indeed, Lady Maclean used the kitchen right up until the conversion was made in the mid-1960s. The food was prepared and cooked in the kitchen, then trundled along the great stone passages on trolleys and loaded onto a service lift to be raised to the dining-room. It's a wonder that any warm food was ever served in Duart, but Jeannie Maclean, who worked there for more than fifty years, says that entertaining was done on a grand scale and there was never any complaint about the quality of the meals. In fact the Banqueting Hall, which was also used as a Drawing Room, was the scene of many parties when hosts and guests would dress in formal highland attire in this most glamorous of settings. Jeannie also remembers that cleaning the castle was a 'bit like painting the Forth Bridge. You started at the top and worked down; when you'd finished, you started at the top all over again.'

At the time of the conversion work, Chips was Chief Scout and was frequently abroad on visits throughout the Commonwealth. As David Mellis recalls:

He came back from one visit to Australia and I greeted him with the words, 'I've just spent £12,000 of your money.' He blanched slightly and then said 'Oh well, I'm sure it will be worth it.' I then went on and spent more than twice that amount before everything was finished to everyone's satisfaction.

Part of the trouble when one opens a place like Duart to the public is that there are certain amenities which have to be installed before you can charge anyone an entrance fee. And because Duart is a private house, public funds were not available as a matter of course. There was a small subsidy from the Highlands Board, which David Mellis describes as 'an encouragement rather than a grant', and they were given a loan of £5,000 by the Board which was repaid over a very short period. However, by the summer of 1968 Duart was ready to open its doors. An attractive tea-room had been built just below the castle and a car park established within walking distance of the main entrance. One additional item of considerable expense was the resurfacing of the road leading to Duart. It's a long, winding, pot-holed single track, but as it provides the only access to the castle it was important that it should be made servicable for the thousands of visitors they were hoping to attract. Finally, after meetings with the Scottish Tourist Board, the National Trust and Macbraynes, who operate the ferry service between Oban and Mull, Duart found itself on the tourist map for the first time.

The first 'paying customers' walked through the Grand Entrance into the Courtyard in June, 1968. They saw the Rowan tree which had been planted to mark the one hundredth birthday of Sir Fitzroy Maclean and, immediately above the double doors, the divided wall which used to house the portcullis. Walking past the massive kitchen they viewed the well hewn out of solid rock which has supplied the castle with fresh water for 600 years, and then they were given a glimpse of what life was like for those unfortunate enough to be taken prisoner in the 16th century. There are two dungeons, each with walls more than twelve feet thick. The first contains a life-like figure of a single prisoner in chains. Two officers from the Spanish galleon *Florencia* which was blown up in Tobermory Bay, in 1588, are incarcerated in the second.

Climbing to the Sea Room they viewed a small cannon salvaged from the sunken galleon, and the bell, wheel and binnacle from RMS *Lochinvar*, the steamer which served the Isle of Mull from 1908 to 1960.

The visitors come from all over the world and they are divided between the usual tourists who are 'doing the Western Isles', and find Duart listed as one of the attractions on Mull, and the Macleans, for many of whom the journey to Duart is a pilgrimage. There are two separate visitor's books; one for the Macleans, the other for the visitors who are not members of the Clan. On a single day in 1985 the page containing the names of the Macleans, included Murial Maclean from Pennsylvannia, USA, Euan Maclean of Victoria, South Australia, Norma Maclean from Enkusen, Holland and Robert Maclean whose address was given as Fairfax, California.

They were greeted by Penny Patrick, the young lady who came to Mull on holiday fifteen years ago – and remained, to marry, settle down and help run Duart. Penny is a vivacious brunette who fell in love with the castle after an afternoon visit with her parents. She wrote to Lord Maclean who had just taken up residence in St James's Palace after being appointed Lord Chamberlain. He invited her to the palace for an interview and since then she has been the main guide and administrator at Duart. A couple of years ago she met and married the manager of the island's main hotel at nearby Craignure and now she divides her time between Duart in the day time and the hotel in the evenings.

She says that for her it was 'love at first sight. I had never been anywhere that attracted me so much, so quickly. In fact after that first short holiday I felt I could never live anywhere else.' For her, showing people around the castle is very much a labour of love, as she says:

Clanspeople will turn up at any time, whether the castle is open or not and we try never to turn anyone away. The Macleans regard this place as their own. They feel they have a proprietorial right to Duart even though most of them have never been here before. We've had Macleans from Japan who arrive knowing more about the castle and its history than we do. Of course the biggest thrill is if Lord Maclean himself is in residence and they can meet him. If he is here, he always turns out in person to greet Macleans and his photograph must adorn more mantleshelves than almost anyone elses. They all love to have a photograph taken with the Chief.

Penny remembers one of the earliest visitors she welcomed when she first came to work at Duart:

He was a very old man who had been brought from his home in Wilton, Iowa, by his son. At the age of eighty-three, he said he had at last fulfilled a lifelong ambition to see the home of the Clan and now he could die happy. He wrote to me for a few years afterwards, and then I heard that he had died – and died content.

Duart is also, perhaps quite surprisingly, a choice for honeymoon couples. Penny Patrick recalls one very wet afternoon when there had been very few visitors:

All of a sudden, there was a banging on the door and there stood two young Americans, who were soaked to the skin. When they removed their raincoats, they were wearing 'His and Her' kilts in the Maclean Hunting Tartan. The bridegroom said that his wife had agreed to marry him only if he promised to take her to Duart on their honeymoon.

One of the favourite parts of the castle for visitors and family alike is the Crimea Corner where uniforms, weapons and other relics associated with Sir Fitzroy Maclean's campaign in the Crimea are displayed, and there's a unique and highly distinctive candelabra which is known in the family as the 'Crimea Trophy'. The silver candelabra comes from the braid of his uniforms and the trophy is mounted on three hoofs taken from one of Sir Fitzroy's chargers that he rode at Balaclava.

There is also a collection of swords containing the 'Chief's Claymore'. This has been worn by successive Chiefs for generations since it was made in Germany in 1690 – it is inscribed with the words 'Stuart von England'.

Visitors who choose the right day in August every year may be treated to a very special sight. It's a long-standing tradition that the Royal Family undertakes a cruise of the Western Isles in August before their summer holiday at Balmoral. For some years it's been the custom of the Royal Yacht to sail close to Duart, when members of the Royal Family come out on deck to wave to Lord and Lady Maclean on the ramparts. Lord Maclean is usually given a few hours notice of *Britannia's* arrival and he always lets off a large number of fireworks in greeting to the Queen and her family. They reciprocate, and the exchange of fireworks between *Britannia* and Duart has become an annual event that's looked forward to by everyone concerned.

And of course Her Majesty not only sails past Duart; she sometimes comes ashore. The Queen is the castle's most distinguished visitor, having been entertained several times, together with the Duke of Edinburgh and other members of the Royal Family.

Duart is not self-supporting. That would be impossible in this day and age. Neither does it make a profit, but it does attract many thousands of visitors every year and the number is growing. If the castle were not open to the public, it would deny to thousands of Macleans a glimpse of their spiritual home and, to others, a unique glance at Scottish history, and that the house would be empty for much of the year.

When the Chief is in residence the castle takes on an additional personality. With Lady Maclean concentrating on the organisation of the tea-room and on her special recipes for soda bread and cakes, which are sold in the restaurant by the young ladies, usually from the Commonwealth, who come each summer to help out, and his Lordship in tartan kilt waiting to welcome the visitors, Duart is a proud union of vivid memories of the past and sharing of the present.

Duart has a history of romance, adventure and tragedy, and perhaps the most evocative corner of this windswept peninsula is the tiny cemetery across the bay from the castle. Here is the grave of Sir Fitzroy Maclean, the restorer of Duart. He is buried facing the place he loved, the place he made into a family home and a home for the Clan.

And perhaps it's not difficult to imagine why there should be this sense of history surrounding Duart. As Lord Maclean says: '1745 isn't all that long ago when you remember that my grandfather who was born in 1835, knew men in his youth, who in their youth could remember the '45 Rebellion.'

Old Sir Fitzroy also had a wry humour in his old age. On the occasion of his one hundredth birthday, he received a telegram from his old adversary and traditional enemy the Duke of Argyll, Chief of the Campbells, suggesting that the centuries-old feud between the Campbells and the Macleans should end. Maclean replied: 'Certainly, for my lifetime.'

Chapter 6

SCOUTING

'Scouting came into my life when I returned to live in Mull after the war,' says Chips, reflecting on the way in which he became involved with the organisation which was to occupy most of his life for sixteen years. He had not had anything to do with the Movement since he was a Wolf Cub as a very young boy in London, and the invitation to take on an official role came as a complete surprise. 'I think they were looking for anyone who was about the right age and who might have a little time to spare,' he says.

The area in which Mull is located were looking for someone to take on the job of District Commissioner and Chips was approached. His response was immediate and positive: 'Certainly not. I know nothing whatever about Scouting and it would be most improper for me to take on such a role and find myself in that position.' The reply came that 'there was not much in it, just the odd visit to camp during the summer and acting as host when Scouts from other districts came into the area.' Chips asked for some literature to be sent to him so that at least he would have some idea of what was expected, and as he says: 'From that moment I was caught.' So he accepted his first public office, that of District Commissioner for the Western Isles of Scotland which included Mull, Coll and Tiree. In the first few years he spent more time actually learning the job than he did carrying out official duties.

There was such a lot to learn and mine was a big area to cover – especially for a new boy. I was sent on a couple of courses to bring me up to date with current standards and I read more books on Scouting in the first two years than I had ever read on anything up until then.

At the same time Chips and his family were trying to get to grips with farming at Duart and re-establish themselves in civilian life. But, as Chips himself comments: 'Scouting is infectious. I know it sounds a very corny thing to say, but the more one got to know about the Movement, the more one realised how much there was to do and the more one became involved.' Chips was to institute sweeping changes to Scouting – but not until he had served his apprenticeship in Scotland before moving to Scout Headquarters in London.

His progress through the Movement in Scotland was fairly rapid. A

few years as District Commissioner, then promotion to County Commissioner, and eventually he reached the highest position in the Movement in Scotland when he became Chief Commissioner.

It was when he was appointed Chief Commissioner for Scotland that
he began to travel to international conferences and he remembers this
period as the first time when he realised that Scottish Scouting was
somewhat different from Scouting in other parts of the United Kingdom. It wasn't that Scouts north of the border did not obey the rules and
regulations laid down by Scout Headquarters in London; but Chips
says, 'They did sometimes put a slightly different interpretation on
certain rules because they felt it would not be appropriate to follow the
English line in every sense of the word.'

In 1958 the Chief Scout was Lord Rowallan. It was he who personally
broke the news to Chips that he wanted him to take over when he
retired. During the annual visit by the Chief to Scotland, 'Billy' Rowallan
was having lunch with Chips at an hotel near Oban before they set out to
tour Argyll. Chips takes up the story:

We went into the dining-room and as we sat down to eat he said,
'There's one thing I want to mention before lunch and it's this. The
Scout Council have decided that they want you to take over from me
when I retire – now let's get on with the soup!' It came as a complete
shock to me because I can honestly say that the thought of one day
becoming Chief Scout had never entered my mind. I thought I had
quite enough to do at home without any further involvement, so I
was not in the least ambitious to more up.

Chips cannot remember much about the remainder of that week; his
mind was in a whirl. Back at Duart he raised the matter with Elizabeth,
who as always was totally supportive. One of the big attractions of the
job was that there was a great deal of travel involved and Chips admits
that 'I have always had a bit of wanderlust.' But as he put it:

That was also something I had to try and disregard. If I had taken the
job solely because of the opportunity to travel the world, it would of
course have been for all the wrong reasons. Then there was the
question of once more leaving Elizabeth and the children for long
periods. We were living at Duart all the year round at this time. We
had no base in London, or anywhere else, so that had to be taken
into consideration.

The idea was that Chips would become Deputy Chief for about
eighteen months in order to make the transition in a reasonable period.
Ultimately, the process was brought forward by a year, because after six
months Lord Rowallan was appointed Governor of Tasmania, which

meant that he had to relinquish his post earlier than he had expected – as Chips would have to, thirteen years later when he was appointed Lord Chamberlain.

One condition Chips imposed was that accommodation would have to be provided in London suitable not only for himself but also for his family. He was not again about to be separated from them from one year's end to another. This was agreed to, and a flat was purchased in Regent's Park. It turned out to be one of the best investments the Scouts had ever made. By the time Chips left the organisation in 1971, the flat was worth more than five times its original price.

The Chief Executive Commissioner of Scouts is Ken Stevens. He is a burly, amiable man who combines the qualities of being an efficient, modern Managing Director with the ideals that have characterised Scouting since the days of Baden-Powell. He is a man with a deep personal faith who, like Chips, actually goes to church every Sunday because he enjoys it.

He first met Chips in 1957 at the World Jamboree which he had organised at Sutton Coldfield. Chips was the Chief Commissioner for Scotland and it was his impact on the international scene of Scouting at this jamboree that Ken Stevens believes was the main reason for his election as Chief Scout two years later. As Mr Stevens says, 'He was very popular throughout the world and he was the unanimous choice.'

The position in Scouting at that time was that the Chief Scout was appointed as Chief of the United Kingdom, and then the leaders of the Movement throughout the Commonwealth were asked if it was their wish that he also became Chief Scout of the Commonwealth. This is what happened in Chips' case and within a few months of becoming Lord Rowallan's successor, he also became Chief of the Commonwealth Scouts. Sadly the unity of the Commonwealth countries has not remained as it was in those days and there is no longer a Common-wealth Chief Scout.

The early days of Chips' reign saw him getting to grips with the complexities of the many different aspects of the Movement, both at home and abroad, and he regards himself as being very fortunate in that the previous Deputy Chief Scout, Sir Rob Lockhart, who was not con-sidered for the top job because of his age, agreed to remain as Deputy to Chips for nearly a year. This was an invaluable aid in the first months, especially as Chips, at forty-two, was the junior by many years of most of the members of the Scout Council.

Within a comparatively short time the new Chief decided that if he was to leave his mark on Scouting he had better get to work fairly quickly. At one of the first national conferences he attended in his new capacity, he spoke about the need for change, for Scouting to keep up with the times. His speech contained a reference to the founder of Scouting, Lord Baden-Powell, and his attitude to Scouting. It reads:

The wheels that made the ruts at Mafeking made the ruts so deep that it is difficult to see over the edge of them – and there are other things than the wheels of Mafeking.

It didn't go down too well with some of the die-hard traditionalists!

But Chips by now realised that there was a need for a shake-up. Most of the older County Commissioners who, like himself when he started, were recruited solely because they were prominent landowners, were dying off and there was a large gap between the middle-aged administrators who were quite happy with the way things were going and the new, younger elements who had returned from the war and who wanted to propel Scouting into the second half of the 20th century. As Chips said: 'It couldn't stand still. It either had to go forward or it would have gone backwards.'

But before he could form the working party that was to consider some of the revolutionary ideas he was to put forward, there were his responsibilities to the countries of the Commonwealth that had to be considered. In 1960 he was invited by the Australian Boy Scouts Association to visit them for a seven-week tour of the country. It was his first visit as Chief Scout and the first time that he had been back since his Public Schools Empire Tour in 1934. Chips has always had a soft spot for Australia and he didn't need much persuading to leave a cold and dismal Britain on New Year's Eve for the sunshine of 'down-under'. His son Lachlan recalled one of his memories of those days: 'Father always seemed to find an opportunity of leaving the country in the worst months of the winter!'

During the next five years Chips' travels would take him to India, Singapore, New Zealand, Kenya, Bechuanaland, Basutoland, Swaziland, Mauritius, Cyprus, Ghana, Tanzania, Canada, Ceylon (as it was then), Hong Kong, Malaya, Zambia and all the other independent countries within the Commonwealth, as well as the United States, Japan and Greece for World Conferences. He toured the islands of the South Seas and went deep into the jungles of North Borneo.

It was during his visit to Singapore that he met Philip Moore, the man with whom he was to work very closely in later years in Buckingham Palace. Sir Philip Moore has just retired as Private Secretary to the Queen, but in those days he was Deputy High Commissioner in Singapore. Prime Minister Lee Kwan Yew was regarded as more than slightly left wing in the early 1960s and when he heard that the Chief Scout was visiting, he let it be known that he was not at all satisfied that the Scout Movement was something he wanted to encourage in the young people of his island. He told Philip Moore that the 'baggy shorts were a reminder of the old British Empire and he didn't want anything to do with that.' Philip Moore relayed this information to Chips before the meeting with the Prime Minister took place, and Chips was able to explain that he was working on a plan which would do away with shorts and that in future Scouts would wear long, tapered trousers more in keeping with modern fashion. Lee Kwan Yew was apparently satisfied and withdrew his objections to Scouting, and today the Movement thrives in Singapore. It was an example of the kind of tactful diplomacy that Chips was to use throughout his career.

There were other newly independent countries where the leaders had doubts about Scouting. Julius Nyere, President of Tanzania had indicated that he was going to ban all forms of Scouting. Chips pre-empted the move by inviting the President to become Chief Scout of Tanzania. Dr Nyere accepted and with the Presidential blessing the Movement went from strength to strength.

One of the strangest meetings took place in the presidential palace in Accra the capital of Ghana. After a long and protracted series of negotiations Chips was finally told he would be granted an audience with President Nkrumah. He takes up the story:

We arrived at the palace to be shown through a series of rooms, each one more intimidating than the last. The murals on the walls all showed the way in which the Africans had thrown off the shackles of the white colonialist oppressors, and the deeper into the palace you went the more uneasy you became. Eventually we arrived in a comparatively small, simple room where the President sat. He was amiable and reasonably talkative and greeted us quite cordially. That evening we were back in the District Commissioner's house where we were staying and there was a reception at which some local press reporters were present. One of them came up to talk to me, and when I mentioned that I had met President Nkrumah that afternoon she said, 'Are you sure it was him?' I replied I had no reason to suppose otherwise and she said that it wasn't always the President one met when one thought one was meeting him. Apparently he had a double who used to substitute for him whenever Nkrumah didn't want to meet anyone face to face. All I know is that I was told it was the President, but I have no way of knowing if it really was him.

There was very nearly an international incident in Malawi where Chips was due to attend a large rally in a football stadium in Blantyre. The local press previewed the event by saying that the Chief Scout would attend 'accompanied by Dr Banda'. That immediately upset the Life President who accepted a secondary role to no one in his own country, and he refused to attend. In fact Chips found Dr Banda to be 'very unhelpful' in his attitude to Scouting. In most of the emerging nations there was a shortage of money for voluntary organisations and the majority of the leaders were supportive. As Chips says, 'Many of them had been educated at missionary schools where there was always a Scout troop attached so they knew all about the Movement,' but Hastings Banda was not interested in providing money for an organisation he regarded as being a hang-over from the colonial power and so Chips' pleas fell on deaf ears.

Whenever Chips went on one of his tours of Commonwealth countries he was accompanied by a single personal assistant and between them they did all the work that would normally take a large retinue to arrange.

Peter Cooke, now retired, travelled with Chips on three of his trips: to East Africa in 1963, Canada in 1967, and India in 1968. It was while they were in Bombay that Chips and Peter had to obtain official forms stating they were both 'alcoholics' in order to buy a bottle of gin from the local chemists. India was dry at the time and the only people who were allowed to consume alcohol were those the government had decreed were genuine 'alcoholics'. As both men liked the occasional gin and tonic in the early evening, they reluctantly agreed to joining the ranks of the 'Admitted Drunkards' temporarily.

Back in Britain, Chips brought modern technology to his aid when he wanted to carry out as many engagements as he could throughout the country. In one two-day period he was able to attend five rallies in different parts of Britain by using a helicopter as a means of transport. It was called 'Operation Touchdown' and it meant that he was able to see, and be seen by, more than 50,000 Cubs and Scouts in the space of thirty-six hours.

However, his use of air transport didn't always go quite as planned. On one occasion he was due to fly with British European Airways from Manchester to London to open the new Scouting Headquarters at Dulwich College. But when he and comedian Tommy Cooper, who was also booked on the flight, turned up at the airport, they were told the flight was overbooked. Chips took the news with his usual calmness and promptly chartered a small, single-engined aircraft to ferry him to his appointment. It cost £50, a substantial sum in those days, and the airline refused to pay, so Chips paid out of his own pocket because he didn't want to let his fellow Scouts down.

Meanwhile Chips' ideas for reshaping the image of Scouting were beginning to take form. He recruited a working party to look into every aspect of the Movement and one of the common factors linking its members was the fact that nobody was over forty-five. It was refreshing to people like Ken Stevens to find that the ideas of young men like himself were going to be given an airing and that no part of Scouting was sacrosanct.

The first meeting of the working party was asked by the Chief if they had thought of changing the Scout Promise – a heresy to those who had grown up with the words of the Founder, Baden-Powell, inscribed on their hearts. Ken Stevens remembers that there was tremendous opposition from some of the older members who believed, like Olave, Lady Baden-Powell, that the Scout Laws had been given to B-P by God, in the same way that Moses had received the Ten Commandments.

And apart from the fundamental changes made to the Scout Laws there were the massive alterations to the image of the Movement. To start with, the change of the old-style traditional uniform; Chips himself was no lover of shorts and his researches proved that the majority of Scouts felt the same way. Another old tradition that the working party decided to do away with was Rover Scouts. They didn't add a great deal to Scouting and it was agreed to disband them and replace them with the more adventuresome Venture Scouts. This was not received with universal approval; some people thought the idea of Rover Scouts was a place where those who had served their time could relax as a reward for past services, but the Chief Scout's 'Advance Party' said 'no'. If they weren't productive, out they went!

Girls were integrated into the Venture Scouts, and when Lady Baden-Powell heard this she was disgusted. She told Ken Stevens, 'My man would never have allowed this to happen.'

When the findings of the Advance Party were published there was a variety of reaction from all over the world. Animal protectionist groups wrote to complain that the law stating that 'A Scout is a friend to animals' had been removed. The answer was that the laws also didn't state that a Scout was a friend to human beings, but it was implicit, so it did not need to be written down.

The tenth law, 'A scout is clean in thought, word and deed,' had also been deleted, but the contents of all ten Scout laws were retained in the main, in the seven laws which were substituted.

Ken Stevens remembers going to see Lady Baden-Powell when she told him that it was a sin to interfere with the laws as written by her husband. He pointed out to her that in fact B-P had written only nine laws; the tenth had been added by the Executive Committee of the Scout Council. 'Nonsense,' she replied, 'all ten laws were handed down to my man from on high.' It was obvious that she really believed that her husband had been chosen by God to lead the young people of the world and nothing would ever persuade her otherwise.

It was a great personal sadness to Chips that, when the Advance Party Report was finished and he had a copy specially bound in leather to be presented to Lady Baden-Powell, she returned it unopened. It remains in Scout Headquarters to this day.

The coolness between the Chief Scout and the widow of the Founder, continued throughout the years Chips was leader of the Movement. It was entirely one-sided because Chips himself desperately wanted to respect Lady Baden-Powell's wishes, and he felt no personal animosity towards her at all. But the needs of Scouting were paramount and the rift between them was never healed. It became public knowledge within the Movement and there was a great deal of surprise in later years when they came face to face at the start of a World Conference. Lady Baden-Powell threw her arms around Chips and said how wonderful it was to see him, to the astonishment of the assembled onlookers; then she whispered under her breath, 'We have to make it seem so, even if it's not true.'

Nevertheless the main recommendations of the Advance Party were accepted even though there were those who felt that parts of the report were a betrayal of all that the Founder had stood for. There was even a break-away movement formed calling itself 'Baden-Powell Scouts'. And some of those troops are still in existence. In retrospect, one or two of the changes were not beneficial and Ken Stevens says that several members of the Advance Party, himself included, now have 'First Class Honours Degrees in Hindsight'. But there was one thing that everyone was agreed upon, and that was that the Chief Scout was becoming as acceptable a public figure throughout the world as any of his pre-decessors. Lord Elgin, an old friend from the Scots Guards, whose stately home is just outside Dunfermline, is President of the Boys Brigade, an organisation seen as slightly competitive with the Scouts. His view on his old comrade's appointment as Chief Scout is fairly typical of the reaction of many people throughout the world. 'Chips brought a Scottish identity to Scouting. Wherever he went he wore his Maclean kilt and in any crowd of several thousand Scouts and Cubs it was easy to recognise him as the leader.' Apparently at one Jamboree, he wore shorts. No one recognised him, so it was back to the kilt for Chips without delay.

Ken Stevens regards Chips as being the 'best Chief Scout I've worked with.' His immediate predecessor Lord Rowallan was also a man with a 'high profile', but as far as the executive workers at Scout Headquarters were concerned he could be somewhat dictatorial. If there was a decision to be made it was invariably made by him, in his own favour, simply because he believed that he knew best. Mr Stevens says that with Chips it was always a case of seeing what the other side of the story was before making any decisions. 'He brought democracy to the executive.'

He was also responsible for the reforming of the Buckingham Palace Cub Pack. This was done to enable Prince Andrew to meet more boys of his own age and those who were invited to join were not just the privileged sons of senior members of the Royal Household.

The pack included boys from modest homes whose fathers were carpenters, plumbers and bricklayers as well as those 'born with a silver spoon in their mouths'.

Chips kept out of the day-to-day running of the Buckingham Palace Pack for obvious reasons. But once or twice he did drop in for a visit and he tells the story of one such evening when the boys asked him 'for a yarn'. He told them the story of Duart Castle and its gory history. One youngster asked if they had a ghost at Duart. Before Chips could reply, another Cub raised his hand and said, 'But there's only one ghost isn't there? The Holy Ghost.' Nine-year-old Prince Andrew offering an unconscious and spontaneous declaration of youthful faith? When the time came for Prince Andrew to go away to his first preparatory school, the Queen indicated that she would like her son to continue his involvement with the movement and Ken Stevens was despatched to the school to see about setting up a Scout Troop. He met with a certain amount of resistance from the headmaster who didn't want to be told what to do by 'any of the parents of his pupils'. It was gently pointed out to him who this particular parent was and he reluctantly agreed, as long as he didn't have anything to do with it. So Scout leaders were brought in from outside and equipment was acquired and stored, and throughout his school career Prince Andrew enjoyed to the full the benefits of Scouting.

Ken Stevens also remembers an incident very early on in Chips' career as Chief Scout, which he regards as an outstanding example of his ability to get on with young people and in particular to pick out those who needed his support. It was during a rally on Epsom Downs which took place in a downpour. When they arrived on the field they were met by 3,000 Cubs all with bright green faces from the dye which had run out of their caps in the rain. Walking among them Chips came upon a line of blind Cubs all patiently waiting to meet the Chief. To the first one he said, 'Pleased to see you', and then immediately realised how inappropriate such a phrase was to blind children. From then on whenever he was introduced to anyone without sight he always said, 'Nice to *meet* you.' He also took off his hat and placing it on the head of the first blind cub told him he was wearing the Chief's hat. Then he placed the crummock he always carried everywhere he went, into the boy's hand and explained what it was and the significance of the staff. The same thing happened with each boy in the line – they couldn't see their Chief, but they could go home and tell their families and friends that they had worn the Chief's hat. He had hit on exactly the right way of giving these handicapped youngsters a special treat they would remember, and Ken Stevens says it was incidents like this that set Chips apart as a Chief Scout.

It was at the same rally that he promised to shake hands with everyone in the camp – all 3,000 of them. What he didn't bargain for was the mischievousness of the young Cubs. As soon as they had shaken his hand they went to the back of the line and joined in again. Eventually he realised it was going on rather a long time and began to recognise some of the faces – the ceremony came to an abrupt end. The Chief didn't mind having his leg pulled but only so far!

Another of Chips' assistants on one of his overseas tours was Graham Coombe, who today is official archivist at Scout Headquarters. He accompanied Chips on the first ever visit by a Chief Scout to the Seychelles in the Indian Ocean. Graham Coombe recalls that the one golden rule that the Chief Scout insisted on was that every evening before going to bed, they had to write their 'thank-you' letters to all the people they had met that day. Sometimes it was as late as one or two in the morning before they got back to their quarters, but Chips demanded a full list of names and addresses from his assistant and then sat down to handwrite his letters.

Another task the assistant had was to remind the Chief of any significant events that required his attention. Things like a special celebration or anniversary in another part of the world would warrant a telegram or message from the Chief Scout, so an accurate diary needed to be kept up to date. One of the problems on a journey such as the one to the Seychelles was that it was impossible to carry anything other than essential luggage. The Chief usually made his visits an occasion for presenting medals and awards to Scouts and Cubs throughout the Commonwealth. Graham Coombe says it was slightly embarrassing on this particular occasion because they didn't have enough room in their baggage to store all the medals and badges they needed. So when the Chief had presented, for example, a Silver Acorn, a hightly prized award, Graham would be despatched to see the recipient and ask for it back so they could present it to the next one in line. All the medals were of course sent from Scout Headquarters after a time, but at least the winners of the awards had the honour of having their prizes presented to them personally by the Chief Scout which would otherwise have been impossible. But such were the economies made when travelling on behalf of the Scout Movement.

It was on the same tour of the Seychelles, that also included East Africa, that Chips and Graham Coombe met Jomo Kenyatta, the President of Kenya. Kenyatta had of course been imprisoned by the British for his activities before his country was granted independence and they approached the meeting with a certain amount of trepidation. There was no need. President Kenyatta proved to be a cordial host and an enthusiastic supporter of Scouting and he gladly accepted a gift of a World Scouting banner which was hung in the presidential palace in a place of honour.

Uganda was also on the itinerary that year and they were welcomed to Scout Headquarters in Kampala before going up the River Nile to Masindi where a large gathering of Cubs were waiting on the river bank all chanting 'Sir Charlie Makalini' – their own highly original pronunciation of the Chief Scout's family name. Of course this was Uganda before General Amin, when Dr Milton Obote was President. Once Amin had gained control in Uganda he appointed himself Chief Scout and it was partly because of this that the Scout Council meeting in Hong Kong in 1971 decided that in future there would not be a Chief Scout of the Commonwealth. There were very real fears that the Ugandan dictator would insist on appointing himself to this role or even to be Chief Scout of the world, as he had already awarded himself the Victoria Cross and many other honours, to none of which he was entitled.

Between December 1960 and August 1971 Chips travelled more than half a million miles and visited seventy-three countries. Some he returned to more than once, such as Australia, New Zealand, Hong Kong and parts of Africa. Others he went to as a delegate to World Conferences, which were held in the USA, Japan and Greece. But the bulk of his overseas work was concentrated in the countries belonging to the Commonwealth and there's no doubt that he regarded his responsibilities to Britain's former colonies and dominions as of paramount importance.

Among those who accompanied him as assistant on his foreign trips was Charles Dymoke-Green. He is a man with a far more impressive Scouting pedigree than Chips himself. He joined the Scouts at the earliest permitted age – eleven – and he has retained his interest and enthusiasm ever since. His father was General Secretary to Baden-Powell himself and he came into frequent contact with the founder as a young man, so his knowledge of the origins of the Movement is second to none.

Charles Dymoke-Green spent most of his adult life in the Far East as a businessman and when the time came for him to retire in 1960, he left his home in Colombo, the capital city of what was then known as Ceylon, and returned to England.

He very soon became involved in the Scouting scene at home and it was during a Scout function that he was introduced to Chips Maclean. There was an immediate rapport between the two men and shortly afterwards when Chips was looking for someone to take on the position of Commonwealth Commissioner it seemed the most natural thing in the world to ask Charles if he would do the job.

Mr Dymoke-Green agreed after a short deliberation and quickly found himself immersed in what turned out to be very nearly a full-time occupation. He organised three overseas tours for Chips; the first to Australia, New Zealand and Hong Kong in 1961-62; then to Southern Africa in 1963, and then back to Australia in 1967 when they also took Janet, Chips' daughter, along as an extra aide. It was her first experience of overseas Scouting and she was totally unprepared for the sight of 5,000 Scouts and Cubs under canvas, everyone apparently determined to shake the hand of the Chief. Janet and the other girls present were outnumbered by five to one, something which she remembers as an ideal situation for a young lady. It was during this tour that Charles Dymoke-Green was witness to an amusing encounter between Chips and a young heavily freckled Scout in Tasmania. When Chips asked him his name, he replied that everyone called him 'Freckles'. The Chief Scout said that was a funny name to be labelled with, whereupon the young man came back like a shot with 'not half as funny as a grown man being called Chips'.

Charles Dymoke-Green believes that the secret of Chips' success is his ability as a communicator. He doesn't speak any foreign languages fluently, but this has never been an obstacle when he wants to get a point across. They were in Hong Kong at Christmastime in 1961 and they went to visit a youth club run by a number of Chinese women, none of whom spoke any English. They had erected a crib showing the nativity scene and there were one or two things that weren't quite right. Chips managed to convey to them the way things should have been, without being able to speak their dialect and without resorting to the classic English way of dealing with foreigners – waving his arms about and shouting at the top of his voice.

One of the most interesting tours they made together was in 1963 when they visited Bechuanaland, Botswana, Lesotho, Swaziland and Mauritius.

Their first stop was at Mafeking, the town forever identified with Lord Baden-Powell after the famous siege during the Boer War. The immediate reaction of Chips and his assistant when they viewed the area from the aircraft as they approached Mafeking was that a more unlikely place for a military siege would be hard to imagine! They were entertained to tea at St Joseph's Convent which had been used as British Headquarters during the siege and met the man who when he was only fourteen years old, had been B-P's orderly at Headquarters.

Charles Dymoke-Green records in his diary that in one village in Bechuanaland, some 700 Scouts, Guides, Rangers and Cubs turned out to meet them 'many of the children being very poorly dressed and looking under-nourished'. He later learned that the girls were better dressed than the boys because in most families the boys were required to work in the fields from an early age and the parents were not as generous to their sons as they were to their daughters, thinking it unimportant for the boys to be well dressed.

The Chief became aware of what he called the 'appallingly high cost' of uniforms for the African children. They were expected to pay between 6/- (30p) to 8/6 (42½p) for a Scout belt. This was far too high considering their family incomes and Chips ordered his assistant to find out if it would be possible to manufacture cheap plastic belts which would serve just as well.

As has already been mentioned, conditions during these tours were sometimes quite primitive, with the Chief and his assistant staying in mud huts from time to time. Most of the time though they were accommodated by hospitable residents such as Seretse Khama and his wife Ruth, the daughter of the former Chancellor of the Exchequer, Sir Stafford Cripps. On one occasion they left their hosts early in the morning to drive to the airport for the next leg of their tour when they passed a small group of Scouts going in the same direction – on foot. When they arrived at the airport, the group turned up only minutes after them, having double-marched seven miles in an hour and twenty minutes – in a temperature somewhere in the upper eighties! They were also to experience the unusual sight and sound of a guard of honour playing the national anthem on mouth organs. In the African bush the ability to extemporise was always to the fore! After an enjoyable 'sundowner' evening – singing round the campfire, one mother told Chips that her small boy arrived home the following morning saying that he had met 'the Chief Scout who has nine million children'.

It is sometimes difficult for Europeans to understand the difficulties under which Scouting exists in some of the under-developed countries and the determination of the Scouts and their leaders to take part in every aspect of Scouting is a salutary lesson to those who live in an affluent society. When a Scout troop at Serronga in Bechuanaland heard that the Chief was going to be at Shakawe for only one hour, they decided they would visit him. To get there, they made a forty-mile river journey by dug-out canoe, taking two days over the trip. But they saw the Chief, each one shook his hand and then, satisfied, they set off back the way they had come. Such was the extraordinary feeling and devotion of these African Scouts in those years in the 1960s.

This charming family photograph was taken in 1953 – Coronation Year – a rather sombre-looking Chips with Elizabeth and their two children, Lachlan and Janet.

The Chief of the Clan 'congratulates the youngest competitor' at the annual Gathering of the Clans at St. Annes, Nova Scotia, Canada.

By the time Lachlan was six years old, the family had moved to Duart to live – and, for most of the year, waterproof clothing was the order of the day.

Janet, The Maid of Morvern, started her role in the public life of Mull at an early age. Here she leads one of her father's prize herd of pedigree Highland Cattle at the Mull Agricultural Show.

He may have been Chief of the Clan and Lord Lieutenant of the County, but he was still a working farmer who had to lend a hand with his herd of long horn Highland cattle. This was the venture Chips later described as 'a very expensive hobby'.

In 1957 the Royal Family took a break during their summer cruise of the Western Isles to picnic ashore at Duart. The children climbing the castle walls are Charles and Anne.

The sun shines as the Queen and the Duke of Edinburgh are welcomed by almost the entire population of Iona, the tiny but historic island just off the coast of Mull.

A day later Her Majesty the Queen arrives at Oban from the Royal Launch, to be greeted by her Lord Lieutenant of Argyll, Sir Charles Maclean. It's easy to see why they say the weather is always so unpredictable in that part of Scotland – this was summer, 1956.

The weather had worsened by the time Her Majesty, and her sister Princess Margaret, had come ashore at Mull – but the rain did nothing to dampen the smiles – or maybe it was simply relief at being back on terra firma.

Cyprus 1963 – and Chips as Chief Scout of the Commonwealth accompanies Archbishop Makarios, President of Cyprus, as he arrives to address the Commonwealth Conference in Nicosia – Chips was never sure if the President was giving an Archbishop's blessing or the Scout salute!

'The Maclean Clan' – Scout Leader Charles Maclean of the 28th Barbados Troop with his two sons, poses with the man who is their Chief in every way.

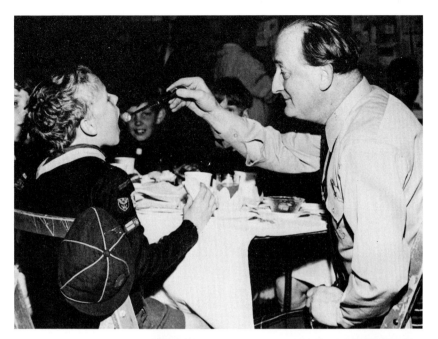

He had a cake in one hand and a sandwich in the other, but he also wanted 'one more strawberry'.

King Constantine of the Hellenes, a life-long supporter of the Scout Movement, receives the Silver Wolf, one of Scouting's highest awards from Sir Charles Maclean. They were to meet many times in the years to come when Chips was Lord Chamberlain.

A Jamboree held in Edinburgh and Midlothian in 1970 where Chips made an important discovery – a blind Cub gets just as much of a thrill in touching the Chief's crummock as his sighted friends do from seeing the Chief in person.

'Is my woggle straight?' – nine-year-old Prince Andrew, a member of the Buckingham Palace Pack, gets a prior inspection from his father, Prince Philip, the Chief Scout and Lady Maclean, before the annual St. George's Day Parade at Windsor.

In Ghanzi a rally was held with 153 Scouts and 166 Girl Guides who had been brought in from outlying villages. There wasn't enough accommodation for them all so an obliging magistrate kindly made the local jail available, the inmates having been transferred to an office building for the night.

In Basutoland the Chief was amazed and amused to find a certain individuality in the uniforms worn by the Scouts. They ranged from a pilot's leather helmet to a Robin-Hood hat of Sherwood green with one or two adding to the dignity of the occasion by wearing skirts over their shorts. On the more serious side there was a real job to be done by the Chief in reassuring the local Chiefs that Scouting was not in any way going to interfere with traditional customs and the local way of life. In Swaziland Chief Ngwenyama, who was reputed to have between sixty and eighty wives, asked specific questions about the Scout uniform. Would it interfere with local dress, and the Scouts' attitude to drinking? He considered alcohol to be the greatest danger to humanity. He also wanted to know what the Chief Scout felt about Communism, obviously thinking that the democratic side of Scouting could lead to an extreme political view in a tribe where the feudal system had been traditional for centuries.

Whenever they travelled throughout Africa, and this was repeated in other tours, Chips was frequently asked to attend Maclean functions. He nearly always refused because as he pointed out, he was not there as Chief of the Clan but as Chief Scout. The programmes had all been worked out in minute detail many months in advance and the only way he could have accommodated the Macleans was by cutting back on his Scouting activities – and this he was not prepared to do. Nevertheless, there were odd occasions when the two coincided and if a Scout turned up who happened to be a Maclean no one was more pleased than Chips.

Towards the end of the tour of African countries in 1963, Chips and his assistant landed in Kenya where Chips found a letter from his son Lachlan who was serving with his regiment, the Scots Guards, in Zanzibar. The letter also contained an air ticket so Chips was able to fly to the island to spend a day with his son – something they found difficult to arrange when they were at home. They had to travel 6,000 miles to find a suitable day on which to meet. It was a pleasant and all too rare oasis in the busy life of the man who led the Scouts of the Commonwealth.

Most of the men who accompanied Chips on his overseas tours said afterwards that he was a good companion, a thoughtful boss and energetic leader, but he was also a perfectionist. He insisted on everything being done properly and he was quick to point out if things were not going as he expected. Peter Cooke says that he was fine as long as the programme was up to date but let things get even a little behind and he would jump on you like a ton of bricks. Graham Coombe says his attention to detail was legendary in the Scouts. He didn't miss a thing and he always followed up any suggestion he made. There was one occasion when he thought it would be a good idea if the assistant took along a supply of 'thank-you badges' for the Chief to hand out. Before the next tour it was Chips who wanted to know if the badges had been included in his luggage.

It was during one of his Commonwealth tours that Chips got the idea of writing to the Prince of Wales who was at that time studying at Geelong in Australia. Chips had never met the Prince, but he thought as he was meeting a number of young people of roughly the same age it might be useful for Prince Charles to hear what they were thinking and to know a little about their living conditions. 'So I wrote a letter, never imagining that I would get a reply. To my complete surprise not only did I get a letter in return, but it was written in his own hand. So as I moved around the Commonwealth I wrote more and more frequently and always received a letter back.' His Royal Highness showed an enormous interest in what was going on throughout the Commonwealth and the two corresponded for many months, until Prince Charles returned to England.

The Prince of Wales told the author that he looked forward to Chips' letters and went on:

I always used to appreciate how when he was Chief Scout he wrote me letters during his Commonwealth tours and kept me in touch with developments in the countries he visited; and in a way which very much enhanced my own enjoyment, both in contacts with the Commonwealth countries and with the Boy Scout Movement.

Another relationship developed when Chips decided to hold a Commonwealth Conference in Cyprus in 1965. He was told that the island's President, Archbishop Makarios, would be willing to address the conference but not in English, and he was not prepared to have an interpreter alongside him. Chips accepted the situation, but was then pleasantly surprised on being presented to the Archbishop to be greeted with the Scout salute – which as many will know is not dissimilar to a bishop's blessing. Chips wasn't sure which he was getting, but then the Archbishop began speaking to the assembled delegates in English, and in the most cordial manner, so all his fears were allayed. Savas Kokkinides was International Commissioner on the island at the time and was responsible for organising the conference. Now retired, he retains an active interest in Scouting and is presently trying to raise money to build an international camp-site at Limmasol. He recalls that Chips went out of his way to meet the rank and file members of the Movement and in spite of the fact that Cyprus is only a small part of the world-wide organisation, Chips made them feel as important as any of the bigger countries who were present.

It was in 1970 when Chips returned from his second tour of Australia as Chief Scout, that he was offered the opportunity of joining the Royal Household as Lord Chamberlain. It meant he had to retire a year earlier that he had intended and there were many loose ends to tie up before he could hand over to his successor.

His thirteen years as Chief Scout had seen a period of vast change. World-wide membership of the Movement had stabilised at ten million, of which 500,000 were in the United Kingdom. He was to be the last Chief Scout of the Commonwealth and his Advance Party had changed the image and the objectives of Scouting fundamentally from those instigated by the Founder, Lord Baden-Powell in 1907.

The word 'Boy' has disappeared from the title 'Boy Scouts', so too had Senior and Rover Scouts to be replaced by Venture Scouts. The Scout Laws were reduced from ten to seven. A Scout no longer had to promise to be 'loyal to the Queen' – the second law merely said 'A Scout is loyal'. And in the public's view the most revoluntionary of all changes: the replacement of shorts by 'tapered, mushroom-coloured, long trousers, without turn-up'. Whatever changes Chips may have been responsible for during his tenure as Chief Scout, many will remember him for this single act. The change of uniform. Is that fair? Ken Sevens thinks it is, simply because it symbolised to the world what Chips was trying to do, and that was to show that Scouting belonged as much to the 1960s as did the Beatles. Chips justified his decision by referring to a referendum among the country's Scouts when the result showed an overwhelming vote in favour of long trousers.

If the world is going to remember him as the man who put the Scouts into long trousers then Chips will accept that decision; perhaps his own singular contribution to the Movement was his 'internationalism'. He travelled more than any of the Chief Scouts who preceeded him, or those who came after. He was totally identified with the Scout Movement throughout the Commonwealth, and indeed beyond it's boundaries. Chips used his own charismatic personality to weld boys and young men from different cultures into a single, cohesive unit with the same objectives, without losing their individuality. By modernising the outlook of Scouting and 'trimming the fat' from the various groups who were hanging on to the out-of-date ritual of the Boer War era, he managed to increase that 'net membership' throughout the Commonwealth.

Not all his changes proved to be beneficial. He admits today that perhaps he went a little too far with some of his radical alterations and that not enough of the 'camp fire, woodsmoke and ging-gang-goolies' remained. The romantic image of Scouting suffered as the more professional approach was encouraged; perhaps there was an over-emphasis on the technical aspects and leaders' academic qualifications.

But the net result was a new, modern, highly trained body of young men whose contribution to the quality of life for those around them would stand them in good stead, not just in the days of the 1960s and 1970s, but also in the 'high tech' years ahead.

As was mentioned at the beginning of this chapter, the present Chief Executive Commissioner of Scouts is Ken Stevens. He has known and served with every Chief Scout since Lord Rowallan. He was a personal friend and confidante of Lady Baden-Powell and knew well her antagonism to the changes being instituted by the Advance Party. Today he is able to say of Chips Maclean: 'He was the best.'

Chapter 7

LORD CHAMBERLAIN

As political democracy flourished in Britain, so the duties of the former members of the Royal Household came to be assumed more and more by members of the political administration. Eventually, the Lord Privy Seal, the Lord Chancellor, the Lord President of the Council, the Treasurer of the Household and the Comptroller of the Household, became political appointments with governmental duties as well as their responsibilities to the Monarch.

The Lord Chamberlain was originally a deputy of the Lord Great Chamberlain, but these days he is completely independent and is responsible for all ceremonial duties relating to the Crown, and is the senior member of the Sovereign's Household.

In 1970 when Chips returned from an extended overseas tour to Australia as Chief Scout, he found a letter waiting for him at his London flat. It was from Lord Cobbold, the then Lord Chamberlain, whom Chips had never met, asking him to contact the Lord Chamberlain's office in St James's Palace. There was no apparent urgency and Chips left for Duart without making contact. When he arrived in Scotland he found another letter from Lord Cobbold, again asking him to get in touch. He recalls:

I telephoned St James's Palace, and spoke to Lord Cobbold who asked me if I would call and see him when I was next in London. I agreed of course, but asked if he could tell me what it was about. He said he didn't want to discuss it on the telephone, but there was something he wanted to tell me and it wouldn't take long. Then I remembered that a friend of mine had mentioned that he was thinking of applying for the job of Master of the Household and I thought that perhaps Lord Cobbold wanted to talk to me about that – whether I knew him well and so on. Anyway, about a week later I went to see him at St James's Palace. It was around five o'clock in the afternoon and I remember going into his office in his apartment which I thought was not very comfortable. In fact I thought it rather stark, with a table and desk with a typewriter on it, and a couple of metal filing cabinets. I had never met Lord Cobbold before, so I did a little homework before I went; discovered who he was, how long he had been Lord Chamberlain and so on. He asked me if I would like a drink. I replied, 'No thank you it's a little early for me.' He then said, 'Well I think you had better have one.' We sat down and without any preamble he said 'I'll come straight to the point. When I retire the Queen would very much like you to take over from me as Lord Chamberlain.'

It was as bare as that – no introductory remarks, no indication of what was to come. I was astounded. I had no idea what the Lord Chamberlain did and I didn't know quite what to say. I told Lord Cobbold that I was Chief Scout and asked what being Lord Chamberlain would involve. He declined to tell me saying, 'I don't want to tell you too much about it; you just go away and think about it for a while. But remember this, when the Queen asks one of her subjects to do something like this, it is very difficult to refuse.'

Within a few days Chips had gone back to Lord Cobbold to find out in more detail what the responsibilities were going to be. Cobbold now went out of his way to explain the duties and procedures, before Chips, who was then Sir Charles, could assume office as Head of the Queen's Household. The first priority was to have him created a Life Peer. The Lord Chamberlain acts as the Queen's emissary to the House of Lords of which he has to be a member. Then Chips would have to relinquish his position as Chief Scout a year earlier than planned, so the Scouts had to be consulted in order that his successor could be found in plenty of time. And of course, Elizabeth's views had to be taken into consideration. In fact it was her response that helped persuade Chips to accept the high honour that was being offered him. Chips says, 'Elizabeth took it completely in her stride, as she has always taken everything else. She had accepted my long and frequent absences abroad as Chief Scout and she realised immediately that our experiences in the Commonwealth would be more than helpful at St James's Palace.'

Once the decision to take the job had been taken, events moved with ever-increasing speed. In the space of three months, Chips resigned his position as Chief Scout; received a two-week crash course from Lord Cobbold in the day-to-day running of the Lord Chamberlain's office; was created a Life Peer and introduced to the House of Lords as Baron Maclean of Duart and Morvern; and presented to Her Majesty, who in turn presented him with his Wand of Office, and invested him as a Knight Grand Cross of the Royal Victorian Order. The Lord Chamberlain is Chancellor of the Royal Victorian Order so he has to be a GCVO in order to sign the warrants awarded to other members.

His introduction to the House of Lords was made doubly pleasurable by the fact that his two sponsors were Lord Wigram, whose family had been friends of the Macleans for many years, and Lord Rowallan, his predecessor as leader of the Scout Movement. Chips remembers:

Everybody was so kind. There was a tremendous amount of work to get through, but friends and colleagues to be, many of whom I had not met before, couldn't have been more helpful. From the moment I stepped into St James's Palace people went out of their way to make me feel at home.

Chips has never discovered who recommended him for the position of Lord Chamberlain. He had known the Queen for some years and had been to Buckingham Palace on a number of occasions as Chief Scout, but at that time he certainly didn't presume to number himself among the Queen's personal friends. And if the offer of the job came as a surprise to him, it was no less a surprise to one or two other senior members of the Household. Lord Charteris of Amisfield is Provost of Eton College, a position he has occupied with distinction since retiring as Private Secretary to the Queen in 1975. When he heard that Chips had been appointed Lord Chamberlain he was both surprised and as he admits today, somewhat dismayed:

His name had simply never arisen. The first thing you do when you are thinking of someone as Lord Chamberlain is look through the reference books at all the Peers. The fact that Chips was not a Lord meant that as far as I was concerned he didn't even come into the reckoning.

In all probability the question of who should succeed Lord Cobbold would have been resolved by the Queen herself, in consultation with her then Private Secretary, Sir Michael Adeane, and the Lord Chamberlain. Certainly Martin Charteris who was Assistant Private Secretary was not privy to any of the discussions that took place and when he heard that Chips had been appointed he felt some reservations about the fact that Chips had no political experience.

I knew that I was about to become Private Secretary when Michael Adeane retired and I was looking for someone who could help me politically, and one thing I knew about Chips was that he knew absolutely nothing about politics. I had nothing against Chips personally who I knew socially quite well; it was just that I didn't think he had the sort of equipment I would have liked the Lord Chamberlain to have when I became Private Secretary.

Subsequently Lord Charteris's fears were completely allayed, and in his opinion Chips became a very successful Lord Chamberlain. And in fact the need for political 'nous' receded and Lord Charteris recalls:

I don't think there was ever a single occasion when I had need of the Lord Chamberlain's advice on political matters and as far as the ceremonial side of the job was concerned, he was absolutely first-class. No one could fault him on any matter of protocol.

Lord Cobbold was a banker by profession and his term of office as Lord Chamberlain coincided with a massive enquiry into the structure of the Civil List, the name which covers the amount of money paid to the Queen and other members of the Royal Family to cover their expenses, and the salaries and expenses of members of the Royal Household. Staff on the Royal Household are paid and pensioned on a basis analogous to that in the Civil Service. Parliament had convened a Select Committee to investigate and report on the need to review the Queen's finances and Lord Cobbold had been instrumental in presenting the case for the Crown. At the time of Lord Maclean's appointment, which was due to take effect in the autumn of 1971, the Select Committee had not completed its task, and so Lord Cobbold was asked to stay on for a few months in case the committee needed any further points clarified before presenting its report. The date of Lord Maclean's appointment was therefore postponed until 1st December, 1971, by which time the work of the committee was finished and the basis of what was to become the Civil List Act 1972 was firmly established.

Other senior members of the Household did not have the same reservations as Martin Charteris and the man who was to become Lord Maclean's closest adviser over the years, Sir Eric Penn, was delighted at the prospect of working with him.

At the time of Lord Maclean's appointment, Eric Penn was Comptroller of the Lord Chamberlain's office, the man responsible for the day-to-day running of all ceremonial and much else regarding the Royal Household. Eric Penn recalls, 'I was absolutely delighted when I heard that Chips was to be the new Lord Chamberlain. I couldn't think of anyone I would rather serve and I knew that he was just the man for the job. I had no reservations whatsoever.'

There are five departments in the Household: the Private Secretary's Office, by far the most important department, in that the Private Secretary is in day-to-day contact with the Queen, is responsible for her programme of events and is her link with Parliament. The Press Office also comes under the Private Secretary and his office looks after all overseas visits by the Queen and indeed the Private Secretary himself always accompanies Her Majesty on all trips abroad.

Then there is the Keeper of the Privy Purse. As the title implies, this office looks after the finances of the Royal Household, not only with regard to the payment of salaries and wages, but also when money is

1977 was one of the busiest years for the Lord Chamberlain with many celebrations of the Queen's Silver Jubilee to organise. The Lord Chamberlain's presence was required at many functions, including the very pleasant task of escorting Her Majesty in St. Paul's Cathedral for the Silver Jubilee Service of Thanksgiving.

One of the many ceremonial duties of the Lord Chamberlain involves the Installation of the Constable of the Tower of London. Here Field Marshal Geoffrey Baker receives the insignia of his office in October, 1975.

Although the Lord Chamberlain is titular Head of the Royal Household, the actual day-to-day running of the Lord Chamberlain's office is left to the Comptroller, Lt. Col. Sir John Johnston, who was not only Chips' right hand for some years, but remains a close personal friend.

In May, 1985 Lord Maclean was honoured by the Queen by his appointment, for the second time, as Lord High Commissioner of the General Assembly of the Church of Scotland. At the Palace of Holyroodhouse, Their Graces posed with members of the Household. The Hon. Mrs Barne, Lord Maclean's daughter, is sitting extreme left, with the Purse Bearer, Charles Fraser, immediately behind the Lord High Commissioner.

November, 1985 and The State Opening of Parliament. Chips'
grandson, Malcolm, helps to carry the Queen's train (he is on her
right) while just in front walks Viscount Whitelaw, Lord President
of the Council.

'A perfect ending to a perfect day' – The Princess of Wales says goodbye and thank you to Chips as she and Prince Charles board the train at Waterloo Station on 29th July, 1981. Chips said afterwards that the kiss was a delightful surprise and he had accepted it on behalf of everyone who had worked so hard to make the wedding day such a success.

required for decorating or building work at one of the Royal homes.

The Master of the Household is responsible for the domestic staff at all Royal residences. There are nearly 200 at Buckingham Palace including one man whose responsibilities include winding all 300 clocks. The Master of the Household also looks after the menus, not only for the everyday meals, but the many banquets, garden parties and formal receptions that take place throughout the year. In addition, the Master of the Household is responsible for the provisions on board the Royal Yacht whenever a member of the Royal Family is on board.

The Crown Equery is in charge of the Sovereign's stables, and is responsible for providing the horses, carriages and motor cars required for processions and for the daily needs of the Royal Family.

The fifth department is that of the Lord Chamberlain's office. The Lord Chamberlain does not run the office himself, in fact his duties are mainly ceremonial. The detailed running of the department is left in the capable hands of the Comptroller, who assists the Lord Chamberlain with the supervision of the Household and his ceremonial duties.

So even though the Lord Chamberlain is Head of the Queen's Household, he does not in practical terms have a department of his own to organise. He oversees all the other sections of the Household, but the administration is left to each individual head of department. The five officers of the Household are equal in status officially, but there's little doubt that the Private Secretary is the man who carries the most weight. His influence is felt by almost everyone, and no Lord Chamberlain who valued his job would dream of trying to interfere with the Private Secretary's duties.

The many functions of the Lord Chamberlain include: carrying out the wishes of the Sovereign in the appointment of Royal chaplains, Royal physicians and surgeons, looking after the internal administration of certain of the other Royal residences, making arrangements for Royal weddings, garden parties, State Visits to the United Kingdom and for communication with Commonwealth countries about ceremonial matters. He superintends the Royal collection of works of art and looks after such disparate positions as the Keeper of the Jewel House, the Master of the Queen's Music, Surveyor of the Queen's Pictures, the Bargemaster and the Keeper of the Queen's Swans. Also he is Head of the Queen's Ecclesiastical Household which consists of the Clerk of the Closet, usually a bishop; the Deputy Clerk; the Dean and Sub-Dean of the Chapels Royal and domestic chaplains and chaplains-in-ordinary, who are concerned not only with the Court, but also by rota, to conduct divine service and preach at Royal chapels.

One of the first things that Chips did after settling in at St James's Palace was to visit every department in the Household to introduce himself – and not just to the senior officials but all the staff from the most junior cleaner up. Lt Col Sir John Miller, the Crown Equerry who has been at Buckingham Palace for more than twenty-five years, remembers Chips visiting the Royal Mews and meeting some of the ladies who sew buttons onto the splendid uniforms worn by the grooms and attendants on the State Carriages:

He was genuinely interested in what they were doing and of course he has this wonderful knack of being able to remember names and faces once he has been introduced. This was revealed on his first Christmas visit around the departments. If he had met someone before he always remembered their names and where they had met. It meant a great deal to the staff some of whom were employed in very humble positions and who rarely saw a senior member of the Household, never mind speaking to them.

Sir Oliver Millar (different spelling from the Crown Equerry) is Surveyor of the Queen's Pictures, and as such is responsible for more than 5,000 works of art in the Royal Collection. He has been working at St James's Palace for nearly forty years where he has enjoyed a distinguished career in a very demanding position. Within two days of Lord Maclean's arrival as Lord Chamberlain, the new Head of the Household turned up in Sir Oliver's room. He introduced himself as Chips Maclean and immediately suggested that Sir Oliver call him Chips, the name by which he had been known to his friends all his life. Sir Oliver could hardly believe his ears. None of Lord Maclean's predecessors had ever been addressed as anything other than Lord Chamberlain or their other titles in all the years he had been in the Royal Household. 'It set the tone of a relationship that was to grow throughout the years we worked together.' He says:

There was no question that Chips was Lord Chamberlain. He looked the part more than anyone I could think of – probably the most dignified figure who had ever occupied that most exalted position. But the friendliness came through right from the start and even though he could give you a real ticking off if you had done something foolish, the fact that you could be on Christian name terms somehow made for a much more relaxed and comfortable working relationship.

Another old friend, the late Col John Harvey spoke about Chips as Lord Chamberlain, shortly before he died in 1985, noting that he brought to the position of the Lord Chamberlain 'a tremendous sense of dignity and responsibility'. Another thing John Harvey remembers is Chips' inflexible attitude to the Royal Family:

My wife and I had been invited to dinner at Chips' apartment in St James's Palace. There were a number of friends from the Scots Guards present and one of them made a facetious remark about a member of the Royal Family. It wasn't too terrible, but it was a little indiscreet. Chips wouldn't have it at all. He demanded an apology immediately – which he got – and as far as I know that man was never invited to St James's Palace again.

Another innovation of Chips' and Elizabeth's was the Waifs' and Strays' Christmas lunches they organised. As the Macleans had no other London residence but their Grace and Favour apartment in St James's Palace, and as Duart was too far to travel for short periods in the winter, they used to remain in the palace throughout Christmas. They discovered that some of their friends were also going to be in London and if they were not going to be with their own families, the Macleans took them under their wing for the holidays. Christmas lunch was a very special occasion when the dignified figure of the Head of the Queen's Household would distribute red noses and funny party hats to all present and nobody was allowed to escape without dressing up. Canon James Mansel was Dean of the Chapel Royal for many years and became not only spiritual adviser to Chips, but also a great friend to every member of the family. He performed the marriage ceremony when their only daughter, Janet, married Nicholas Barne, another Scots Guard, and after Canon Mansel's wife died, the Macleans made sure he was included in many functions and parties; a gesture he has never forgotten. He remembers with great affection the Christmases he spent with them and says, 'If it wasn't for Chips and Elizabeth, I would have spent a very lonely retirement.'

On the business side of the job, Chips was learning as he went along. There was no official 'job description' to help an incoming Lord Chamberlain, and it was the discreet help of his colleagues that was the greatest assistance.

The funeral of the Duke of Gloucester in 1974 was one of the earliest Royal funerals to be televised and Chips, accompanied by Sir Eric Penn, went over every detail many times before the ceremony. He recalls that on one occasion they were in St George's Chapel at Windsor Castle where the funeral service was to be held and were discussing with the television producer where the cameras should be cited. 'The producer wanted to put one camera right in the centre of the central aisle about half way down. I said that would never do – the people sitting behind wouldn't be able to see a thing. It was quietly pointed out that if the camera wasn't located where the producer wanted, ten million people watching at home wouldn't be able to see a thing. He got his way.' It was observations like this that became invaluable to the Lord Chamberlain and which were to stand him in good stead in future years, when he would be responsible for some of the biggest media events ever, such as the Queen's Silver Jubilee celebrations in 1977, the Queen Mother's 80th birthday service in St Paul's in 1980 and of course, the biggest television event of the century, when the Prince of Wales married Lady Diana Spencer in July, 1981.

One task he was not called upon to undertake was that of official censor, which had been the responsibility of the Lord Chamberlain since the 16th century. His predecessor Lord Cobbold had enjoyed, if that is the right word, the power of deciding what was right and proper to be seen and heard in public performance and had had occasion to ban three most distinguished playrights: John Osborne, Joe Orton and Arthur Miller. But in 1968 The Theatres Act became law and all censorship finished in Britain. Nevertheless copies of the banned plays and scripts remain in the cellars at St James's Palace and there was nothing to prevent Chips from browsing through them if the fancy took him.

Until recently, Vice Admiral Sir Peter Ashmore was Master of the Queen's Household and he came to Buckingham Palace just a year after Chips. He was welcomed by the Lord Chamberlain and then left to get on with his job on his own. He says 'I think that was the strength of the way Chips ran the Household. He didn't interfere. He was always around if you wanted him, but he allowed one to get on with the job in one's own way. It was very nice to know that if you needed advice he was there – it was a bit like being a referee. As long as you obeyed the rules he kept quiet, but if you once overstepped the mark, he would blow the whistle.'

Like most of the other heads of department in the Royal Household, Peter Ashmore didn't see a great deal of Chips on a day-to-day basis, but there were occasions when the Lord Chamberlain was called upon to arbitrate if there was a dispute. Peter Ashmore recalls:

There was one case when I wanted to fire a man who worked in the stores. I discovered that he was very dishonest. The problem was this man had worked at the Palace for more than twenty years and indeed he had been awarded the MVO by the Queen. The Keeper of the Privy Purse took an opposing view and argued that he should not be sacked in view of the length of his service. There was a very acrimonious row and neither of us would give way. Eventually Chips was asked if he would investigate and made a decision. It was an extremely delicate mission and I felt so strongly that I was prepared to resign if the man in question stayed. Chips came to see me in my room (it's the same room that Michael Fagan used to gain entry to the palace when he was arrested in the Queen's bedroom) and I gave him my side of the story. Then he continued his inquiries throughout the palace. I actually never heard another word about the matter, but the man left.

It was an example of Chips mixing his own unique brand of diplomacy with office politics. There was no great fuss and no official decision published, just a great deal of commonsense applied by someone who had by then become used to the intricacies of life in the corridors of the most famous house in the world.

There was another occasion in which, this time, the Lord Chamberlain decided not to get involved. Again the two protagonists were the Master of the Household and the Keeper of the Privy Purse. Visitors to Buckingham Palace are admitted by the Privy Purse entrance – it's the door on the extreme right as you look at the palace from the front. The door will be opened by a footman wearing a scarlet waistcoat and a dark green tail coat. To the right of the entrance is the waiting-room where visitors are asked to sit until they are guided to the room of the person with whom they have an appointment – no one is allowed into the palace without a prior appointment. The waiting-room contains a writing-desk (without any notepaper), a marble-topped table on which rest copies of *The Times* and the *Daily Express* and a number of gold-painted chairs and one sofa which are covered in lime green silk. On the walls are two paintings by the Victorian artist W P Frith: 'Departure Scene, Paddington Station' and 'Life at the Seaside'.

Normally one waits only for a few minutes before being taken to see whoever is expecting you. But it's a pleasant room in which to while away the time and a gentle introduction to the splendours that lay within. Until the mid 1970s, visitors were required to wait in a tiny claustrophobic closet, and because of this Sir Peter Ashmore decided that improvements were needed. So he proposed that a new waiting-room should be constructed with the money that was available from that year's annual estimates in the Royal Palaces vote. 'The money was there,' said Ashmore, 'so there was no reason why the work couldn't be done.' But there were strenuous objections from Sir Rennie Maudsley, Keeper of the Privy Purse, who said that money should not be seen to be spent, with the country at that time in one of its periods of financial crisis. But that wasn't the real reason according to Peter Ashmore: 'The new waiting room would have been right outside Rene Maudsley's door and I'm sure he didn't relish the thought of all that building work going on for six months. Anyway we couldn't get the thing resolved so I asked

Chips to step in. He refused, saying he wasn't going to come down on one side or the other.' Eventually the matter was decided by the Queen herself – and the reason why visitors are able to sit in comfort these days, is due entirely to the fact that Her Majesty told Peter Ashmore to 'go ahead'.

In the thirteen years that Chips was Lord Chamberlain there was only one tragedy that had to be reported to him. This was when a young housemaid committed suicide at Buckingham Palace over a love affair that went wrong. Peter Ashmore was the girl's superior in that he is responsible for all domestic staff, but as Head of the Household, the Lord Chamberlain had to be informed, and in any case it certainly wouldn't have done for him to read about it in the newspapers without having prior knowledge.

Within six months of taking office, Chips was called upon to exercise the greatest tact and diplomacy when he organised the funeral service of the Duke of Windsor. On 28th May, 1972, the former King Edward VIII died in Paris. After nearly forty years in exile he was finally accorded, in death, a ceremonial homecoming. The Duke had asked to be buried at Frogmore, not in the traditional resting place of Sovereigns of the House of Windsor, the crypt of St George's Chapel within the boundary walls of Windsor Castle. His body was flown to England and two days later, his widow arrived in an aircraft of The Queen's Flight that had been sent specially to Paris to collect her. All the arrangements for the funeral were made by the Lord Chamberlain's department; for Chips it meant walking a tightrope for the few days that the Duchess stayed at Buckingham Palace. Throughout the years of her marriage, the Duchess was denied the right to be addressed as 'Your Royal Highness' and the Lord Chamberlain, who accompanied the Duchess to Heathrow Airport, from where she was to fly back to Paris, had to remind himself of the fact and also remember not to bow as he bade her farewell on behalf of the Queen – only those recognised as Royalty receive bows and curtseys in the United Kingdom. Chips remembers very clearly the last car ride from Windsor to Heathrow:'The Duchess was very small, very composed – and there wasn't the hint of a tear.'

1972 had both it's tragic and happy times for the Royal Family. As well as the death of the Duke of Windsor there was also the untimely death of the young Prince William of Gloucester in an air crash, at which time Lord Maclean's future son-in-law was his equerry; but there were also the celebrations of the twenty-fifth wedding anniversary of the Queen and the Duke of Edinburgh. Then the following year, 1973, came the first of Lord Maclean's major television spectaculars, the wedding of Princess Anne and Captain Mark Phillips.

Although the wedding was not a State Occasion, there were some

1,800 guests invited to the service in Westminster Abbey and an estimated television audience of some 500 million watching throughout the world. It was the first Royal Wedding seen in colour and Princess Anne's wedding did for the sales of colour televisions sets, exactly what her mother's Coronation had done for the sale of the old monochrome sets in 1953.

The Lord Chamberlain was made responsible for all the wedding arrangements including the approval of the many souvenirs which were produced to mark the occasion. 'Some of the suggestions were not always in the best taste,' he remarks with commendable understatement. Although each department in the Royal Household operated with a great deal of autonomy, there were a number of occasions when it was necessary for policy meetings to be held regarding the entire Household; these were always held under the Chairmanship of the Lord Chamberlain. For example, whenever there was a State Visit expected, he would summon all the senior members of the Household plus Police, Transport, Airport Officials and representatives of the Services to St James's Palace to finalise the details. There was never any doubt in anyone's mind who was in charge and Sir Peter Ashmore says that his attention to the smallest detail was remarkable. He knew exactly who should be doing what, and if they weren't, he wanted to know why.

As Chancellor of the Royal Victorian Order, Chips held a meeting twice a year to discuss promotions in the order. This is of course the Sovereign's personal order of chivalry and all awards are made solely by the Queen herself. Martin Charteris remembers attending those meetings regularly and feels that it was in this context that Chips was at his best:

He was so completely honest at all times. Probably the straightest man I have ever known. He handled the meetings very well and whenever a name was mentioned Chips had always done his homework, so he knew everything there was to know about that person and he insisted on a full discussion of every case so that his recommendation to the Queen could be unequivocal.

Unlike all other honours, the recipients of the Royal Victorian Order are not told in advance. If someone is to be awarded an MBE, a Knighthood or made a Life Peer, they will normally receive a letter from the Prime Minister's office about six weeks before the date of the award, telling them that 'The Prime Minister has it in mind to recommend the award . . .' That way the recipient can indicate if he or she is willing to accept and there is no embarrassment if they wish to refuse. The recipients of any grade of the Royal Victorian Order first know about it when they read the announcement in the press on the morning of the award. This was the case with Sir Henry Clowes, an old friend and comrade of Chips who had served with him in the Scots Guards during the war.

Sir Henry was a member of the Honourable Corps of Gentlemen at Arms which is made up of retired senior Army officers who are on duty at all Royal occasions such as the State Opening of Parliament, all State Banquets and Garden Parties, where they are responsible for organising 'the lanes' down which members of the Royal Family walk. During the time when Chips was Lord Chamberlain, Sir Henry Clowes was Clerk of the Cheque and Adjutant to the Honourable Corps, and came into frequent contract with his old comrade in arms. Early one morning he was awakened to be informed by another friend that he had been awarded the CVO in the Birthday Honours List published that day. It was the first he had heard about it and naturally he was delighted at the news. It was a day for double celebration in the Clowes family because they already knew that Lady Clowes had been awarded the OBE for public service in the same Honours List. When the day of the investiture came, Sir Henry and his wife were thrilled to find that they were to be presented to Her Majesty at the same time. Chips had found out about the double honour and had arranged that husband and wife would receive their awards from the Queen together – an extremely rare occurrence. Sir Henry and his wife both remember with gratitude this kindly gesture on the part of their old friend and colleague.

One of the early problems that Chips had to cope with was establishing a work pattern. He was the first 'full-time' Lord Chamberlain for many years. Both his immediate predecessors, Lord Scarborough and Lord Cobbold had retained other interests, and homes in other parts of the country, so they were not seen around St James's Palace nearly as often as Chips. He describes a typical day in the working life of the Lord Chamberlain:

I usually went into the office around ten in the morning. This might seem a rather late hour to start work, but the reason was, I had to give the other members of the staff time to open all the post and sort out what needed to be seen by me before I got there. Then I would probably have a session with either the Comptroller or the Assistant for half an hour or so, and then leave the palace for one of the outside duties. This could be a visit to the Tower of London to make my annual inspection of the cleaning of the Crown Jewels by the Crown Jeweller. This was a fascinating job and I was always amazed to see these famous crowns being taken apart and jewels like the Black Prince's ruby being handled just as if it was a half-crown piece. We had to take particular care to see that the cases in which the regalia is displayed were always in first-class condition; the lights placed so that the items were shown to their best advantage and the air-conditioning kept at just the right temperature so that the precious stones and metals were not damaged in any way. Most of the ladies and gentlemen who clean the regalia have been doing it for more than twenty years and they take a great pride in their jobs. Then I would go to Buckingham Palace for lunch at least twice a week. I thought this was important because it gave other members of the Household a chance to nobble the Lord Chamberlain over a glass of sherry if there was a particular topic they wanted to raise.

The pre-lunch drinks are served in the Equerries Room on the ground floor of the palace and Chips thought the venue ought to be changed:

There we were enjoying our drinks before lunch with perhaps the Queen's Equerry sitting at his desk trying very hard to cope with a complicated programme for that afternoon's time-table, while all the talk was going on around him. I thought it must have been distracting, so I suggested to a couple of my colleagues that we move to another room. I was soon put in my place – in a charming manner. It was pointed out to me that a sharp-witted Equerry who kept his ears open could pick up all sorts of useful information in the half hour before lunch and that they liked the status quo and wanted it to remain. I was told: 'They enjoy it – don't interfere.'

It was during Chips' time as Lord Chamberlain that the practice of paying for lunch was introduced, something of which he approved:

It was felt that we should contribute something because the staff canteens 'below stairs' had had their charges increased slightly. After all we enjoyed excellent food cooked in the Royal kitchens by the Royal chefs. We also had to tick off on a list the number of drinks we had. Beer was free, but we paid for spirits. I noticed that the consumption of alcohol dropped considerably which was no bad thing, so the charges were well justified.

There was no formal seating plan at lunch but there was usually one place with a small silver bell alongside to summon the next course. This was reserved for the Lord Chamberlain or the Master of the Household, but Chips rarely used the place. He preferred to move around the table so that he could sit next to various members of the Household in turn.

Then in the afternoon it was back to St James's Palace to deal with correspondence for a few hours and perhaps sort out some diplomatic problems with the Marshall of the Diplomatic Corps whose office was next door to the Lord Chamberlain's. Lord Michael Fitzalan Howard was Marshall of the Corps for much of the time that Chips was in office, and he had a few ticklish problems to resolve with regard to the protocol involved when members of the diplomatic corps were to be invited to a palace function. He told me:

There is a definite pecking order among the 149 Diplomatic Missions in London and procedure is strictly adhered to in order of the number of years each Head of Mission has been in London. It makes no difference if the country concerned is one of the major powers, the order of the priority depends entirely on how long the Ambassador or Head of Mission has served in the capital. Some diplomats would ask for invitations for all their staff to accompany them to a particular function and it required a great deal of tact to explain that there simply wasn't enough room to accommodate them all.

The biggest event of the diplomatic year is the Evening Reception given by the Queen at Buckingham Palace in November for all members of the Corps Diplomatique, when envoys of every country represented in London are invited to a splendid gathering. As Michael Fitzalan Howard remarked: 'Everyone is on parade that evening, wearing every "rock" in the book – especially those from the "Iron Curtain" countries.' But the Lord Chamberlain's presence was also required at a small number of functions which were not of the Royal variety. Whenever a long serving member of the Household was leaving, a reception or dinner would be given in his honour and the Lord Chamberlain invariably attended in person and offered a few 'well chosen words of thanks'.

On three or four nights a week there might be a formal dinner party given by Lord and Lady Maclean for an Ambassador or High Commissioner when they would also invite one or two close friends to help make up the party. Colleagues in the Royal Household feel it was on such occasions that Lady Maclean came into her own. Sir Alistair Aird, Equerry to Queen Elizabeth, the Queen Mother, lived next door to the Macleans in St James's Palace and he and his wife were often guests in their apartment:

Elizabeth was so good at arranging parties, particularly when there was an Ambassador or High Commissioner from one of the under-developed countries. Perhaps he and his wife had not been in London before and they were a little at a loss at first. She soon put them at their ease and introduced them into the social round and made sure the wives in particular were never neglected.

Other functions that involved the Lord Chamberlain included 'Swan-Upping'. This is a centuries-old custom whereby all swans on a stretch of the River Thames between Sunbury and Pangbourne are marked as being the property of the Queen or one of the two Livery Companies of the City of London to whom all swans in Great Britain belong. The Livery Companies are the Vintners and the Dyers and, once a year, their representatives together with the Lord Chamberlain set out in boats along the Thames looking for swans which have not been marked. Whenever a cob and hen with a group of cygnets are sighted, the cry 'Up,Up,Up' is heard and the group is herded into the bank of the river where the cygnets are then marked. If there are four for example, two would be marked for the Queen, and one each for the Livery Companies.

The Office of Keeper of the Queen's Swans has resided in the Turk family of watermen for generations and the 'Uppers' – the men who actually catch and mark the swans – are very fit, experienced boatmen who row a four-man scull alongside the motor launch containing the Lord Chamberlain and his colleagues. On one occasion Chips was rash enough to reveal that he had done some rowing at school. Whereupon he was invited into the scull by the watermen who were determined to have some harmless fun at his expense. So Chips, who occupied the 'stroke' position in the boat, began at a leisurely pace. He soon found that the men behind him were quickening up the pace to see how well he would last. Eventually he 'caught a crab' as they knew he would and Russell Wood, another of the Queen's Household, who happened to have his camera handy, captured for all time, the sight of the Lord Chamberlain, flat on his back with his legs in the air as he tried to regain some sort of composure and dignity. But as Chips says, 'It's a lovely day out on the river.'

Twice a year the Queen invites an overseas Head of State to stay at Buckingham Palace or Windsor Castle and the Lord Chamberlain is responsible for making all the arrangements for the ceremonial functions during the State Visit. Chips revealed:

The first function is always the lunch on the opening day. It's an 'ice-breaker' when both sides are able to get to know one another. Some of the visiting Heads of State and their entourages are very nervous when they first come to Buckingham Palace or Windsor, especially when they see the Gentlemen at Arms and the Yeomen of the Guard in their splendid uniforms.

Then on the first night there is always a State Banquet in honour of the Chief guest and this is when the Lord Chamberlain has to perform one of the trickiest operations of his career. He has to walk backwards, facing the Sovereign, as the Royal procession enters. Chips says there are three rules to follow when you have to walk backwards in front of the Queen:

The first is to practise as often as you can. It's no good thinking, 'I've done it before so it will be alright this time.' The Lord Steward, who walks beside me, and I used to spend a lot of time actually rehearsing the walk before each occasion. Second, the pattern on the carpets are seldom altered in the Ballroom at Buckingham Palace or St George's Hall at Windsor where the banquets always take place, so we got to know the pattern rather well and which seam to follow. The third thing to remember is to watch the Queen. I am only a few feet in front of Her Majesty and she would guide me if necessary, so if I started to wobble a bit, she would gently motion with her eyes, left or right to put me back on the right track.

It was a bit more difficult at Windsor than Buckingham Palace, because at the Palace the Lord Chamberlain and the Lord Steward would walk side by side, while at Windsor, they would be at either side of the long table in St George's Hall. Chips recalls that during President Reagan's visit, which was not regarded as a State Visit even though there was a great deal of ceremonial attached to the functions, he, Chips, was preceeding the Queen into St George's Hall, with the Lord Steward on the far side of the table, when her Majesty muttered to him under her breath, 'You're going to win by a short head' – to indicate that he was getting too far ahead of the Lord Steward.

Another point one had to watch all the time was how long it took the Royal procession to walk from the entrance to their appointed places. The National Anthem is always played whenever the Queen enters the Banqueting Hall and it has to finish as she reaches her chair. This means two verses at Buckingham Palace and one verse at Windsor. So Chips would discuss with the Director of Music how long the procession was going to take – and then make sure he paced himself accordingly. There was only one occasion when things threatened to go wrong and that was at Windsor. 'It was at the end of the meal,' he says, 'and when the Queen rose, so too did everyone else of course, but they failed to move their chairs back, which meant I could not follow my usual seam along the carpet. There was a certain amount of negotiating, but in the end all was well.'

It was moments like this that made him think occasionally: 'Perhaps this could be a good time for there to be a Court Jester, as well as a Lord

Chamberlain.' A good point to make!

In Chips' opinion it was the never-failing good humour of the Queen herself which saved the occasion many times: 'Her Majesty was always ready to smile at some awkward moment or slight lapse so long as no one was embarrassed.' But apparently the Duke of Edinburgh was not quite as accommodating if things went wrong. There was one occasion when the Queen and the Duke were returning to Buckingham Palace after the State Opening of Parliament during which the Lord Chamberlain is always required by law to remain in the Palace 'to await the safe return of Her Majesty'. On this day the lights had failed just before the Royal couple came back, so Chips apologised to the Queen who was fully understanding. Prince Philip though was not amused and asked, with some asperity, why the reserve generator had not been brought into use immediately.

And it was Prince Philip who always used the same words to the Lord Chamberlain on these occasions: 'Look after the place, Chips'; and when the Royal couple returned to the Palace after the State Opening of Parliament, he invariably said, 'Glad to see it's still here, Chips.'

The dignity of the office of Lord Chamberlain has to be maintained at all times, but sometimes it helps to have a sense of proportion – and a dash of humour also comes in handy. One instance where this was superbly demonstrated occurred during the annual inspection of the burial vaults at Windsor Castle. The reason why every Royal occasion appears to go without the slightest hitch is the continual attention to detail by the members of the Household who have responsibility for the various functions.

One of the Lord Chamberlain's duties involves the burying of members of the Royal Family, except the sovereign, the Earl Marshal looks after that. During the rehearsal for the funeral of the Duke of Gloucester, Chips accompanied by the undertakers, who have held responsibility for these matters for many years, was inspecting the arrangements at Windsor. He was dressed in a short black jacket and striped trousers, as was the custom.

There were three Guards officers also in civilian clothes and Chips overheard one of them ask his companions, 'Who's the little fellow with the round face?' To which the reply was 'Oh, I expect he's one of the undertakers.' The Lord Chamberlain did not enlighten them then, but their faces when they found out at the actual ceremony, must have brightened an otherwise depressing duty!

Chips' interest extended to all aspects of life in and around the Royal palaces. In particular he took a special pride in the chapels where both he and Elizabeth were regular worshippers. Anthony Caesar is Sub-

Dean of the Chapel Royal and when he first arrived at St James's Palace as Sub-Dean he was made welcome by the Lord Chamberlain and his wife. He says:

It is impossible to think of one without the other. Whenever I mention Chips, I automatically include Elizabeth. I remember in my early days they were absent from church one Sunday morning. I received a handsome apology from the Lord Chamberlain who used a nice old-fashioned phrase not often heard today: 'I love my church.'

But he would also point out any lapses he felt needed to be corrected. Anthony Caesar remembers that Chips 'liked to see things done decently and in order, so if he had noticed that the hair of a choirboy was unkempt, he would mention it – and make sure it didn't happen again.' Canon Caesar feels that:

Doubtless it was part and parcel of the office of Lord Chamberlain to be observant of such things, but it was also in the nature of the man himself; he was one of those people who led by personal example so that one was inspired to produce the very best.

He had an affectionate regard for the Children and the Gentlemen of the Choir of the Chapel Royal and occasionally he would invite the gentlemen to provide musical light relief when he was entertaining distinguished visitors in his private apartments at St James's Palace. This became well known and extremely popular. On at least one occasion just at the singers were preparing to leave, Princess Margaret, who was a guest asked for more – they were delighted to oblige.

Perhaps it was as a result of his natural ability to establish a rapport with the young that he continued, when Lord Chamberlain, to maintain friendly relations with the children of the Choir of the Chapel Royal. When retirement came in 1984, the Head Boy of the Choir, Laurence Glynn, who was twelve years old at the time, wrote this tribute in the *Chapel Royal Magazine:*

Lord and Lady Maclean both take a lively interest in the Chapel and the Children of the Chapel Royal . . . We all appreciated the thoughtful way he always came to congratulate us when he thought that we had sung particularly well in a service. Lady Maclean succeeded in providing the most delicious cakes for our Christmas party. They will both be missed at Chapel . . .

The Very Rev Michael Mann is Dean of Windsor and Domestic Chaplain to the Queen. He lives in a charming house within the castle walls alongside St George's Chapel, which contains, in his study, a long refectory table on which was laid the body of King Charles I after his execution, and it was on this table that the severed head of the monarch was sewn back onto the body, before it's burial.

Michael Mann came to the priesthood comparatively late in life. He had been a career soldier and retired at the age of thirty-two as a Major in the Queen's Dragoon Guards – the same regiment as Captain Mark Phillips. He was ordained after leaving the Army and quickly rose to become Bishop of Dudley before being appointed to the Royal Household. He assesses the character of Chips Maclean in a particularly perceptive and astute manner:

As far as I am concerned his main characteristic was his integrity. I cannot imagine him being capable of a mean or nasty deed. Neither could I conceive of him telling a lie. Perhaps in this day and age he was too honest for the job. The Royal Household is one of the most competitive places in the world with everyone jockeying for power, which in this instance means access to the sovereign and Chips simply refused to compete. Luckily he didn't have to because of his unique talents but in a lesser man it could have meant going under.

His gentleness could be deceptive, though, and Michael Mann recalls one chapter of events in which Chips played a leading part and which resulted in the Dean remaining in Royal service when things could have gone the other way. In 1979 it was put to Michael Mann that perhaps he had overstayed his welcome in the Royal Household and that the Queen felt his talents would be best used elsewhere. The information had come from sources outside the palace but within ecclesiastical circles. He was dismayed to hear the news because as he put it: 'I do not have private means and I need to stay in this job until the retiring age of sixty-five in order to qualify for a pension.'

He found himself in a quandary. On the one hand he didn't feel he should stay on if it was the Queen's wish that he should go, and on the other hand he wasn't at all sure that his informants were relaying the true wishes of Her Majesty. There was no way in which he could approach the Queen herself to verify the truth of the story, so he needed someone to act on his behalf. The one person he felt he could trust completely on such a delicate matter was the Lord Chamberlain. He asked Lord Maclean if he would ask the Queen what her wishes were. Chips, choosing his moment with care, raised the subject with both the Queen and the Duke of Edinburgh, whose correspondence with Michael Mann on spiritual matters has since been published in book form. The reply he received was that both Her Majesty and His Royal Highness were perfectly happy with the religious guidance being given to the Royal Family and they would be delighted if he would remain in their service 'for the full extent of his time'.

Chips passed on the message to the Dean who received it with gratitude and relief. It was one of the most difficult problems to deal with and required the utmost tact and delicacy – and the services of a completely honest man. The Dean is still in Royal service, a fact he feels is due entirely to the good offices of the former Head of the Queen's Household. If there was one aspect of the job of Lord Chamberlain that Michael Mann would have changed, it would have been to encourage Chips to involve himself more in the day-to-day running of the various departments within the Household. He felt that Chips held back partly because so many of the senior members of the Household had been there for many years and were on more intimate terms with the Queen than he was himself. People like Sir John Miller, the Crown Equerry, were not only servants of the Queen, but close personal friends, so it was fairly easy if he wanted to talk to the Queen about something to do with horses. He would simply ring her up direct. Lord Maclean never felt in that position. He saw Her Majesty a couple of times a month on official business but always by appointment, by ringing the Royal Page first. There was no question of the Lord Chamberlain sticking his head around the door of the Queen's room or just popping in for a chat.

Sir John Johnston feels that it was probably Chips' background in the Scots Guards that helped to make him such a successful Lord Chamberlain:

He has this tremendous eye for detail, particularly with regard to ceremonial and I feel this could only have come from someone who had served in the Brigade of Guards. His Predecessor Lord Cobbold had come from a different background and never involved himself in the detail of the ceremonies we organise. He kept away much more than Chips and left everything to the office, whereas Chips wanted to know every detail and of course he was extremely knowledgeable.

Perhaps it was also his Guards background that prompted him to take a keen interest in the soldiers who stand guard on the Royal residences. Chips remembers one dark night when he happened to look out of his window at St James's Palace and saw a small red glow coming from within one of the sentry boxes. He immediately left his room and walked up to the sentry suspecting that the man had been smoking on duty. He spoke to the soldier and told his of his suspicions. There was no reply – as any passer-by will know, the sentries never acknowledge by word of mouth, any comments made to them when they are on sentry duty. Chips says:

I stood there for about fifteen seconds which must have seemed an eternity to the sentry. Then finally he had to let his breath out and I was enveloped in a cloud of cigarette smoke. I thought the poor chap had suffered enough by then so I didn't report him or mention the matter to anyone. It was enough that he knew that I knew.

There was another occasion when Chips was on the receiving end. The night before an investiture was to take place at Buckingham Palace, he tripped over a paving stone and by the following morning he was sporting two magnificent black eyes. Now at an Investiture, the Lord Chamberlain stands slightly behind the Queen and to one side and reads out the citations of those who are to receive awards. Chips turned up for duty wearing his morning dress, the Band of the Household Brigade was playing selections of music during the ceremony and Her Majesty carried out the whole proceedings immaculately, with only the slightest twinkle in her eye each time she caught sight of her Lord Chamberlain looking as if he had come off second best after three rounds with the Crown Equerry.

John Titman is Secretary of the Lord Chamberlain's Office and is one of only two members who were serving in the reign of King George VI (the other is Sir Oliver Millar, Surveyor of the Queen's Pictures). He first met Lord Maclean when he was appointed Lord Chamberlain and has always addressed him as Lord Chamberlain or Lord Maclean, never Chips. There is a subtle dividing line in the Royal Household between Members and Officials; Members always refer to each other by Christian name but to Officials by their surnames.

John Titman has responsibility for a great deal of detail surrounding Royal ceremonial. On the day I met him in his spacious office in St James's Palace he was preparing the schedule for the new Lord Chamberlain, Lord Airlie, to hand over the Keys of the Tower of London to the incoming Governor of the Tower. Mr Titman says the main difference between Lord Maclean and his predecessors was that Lord Cobbold, and before him Lord Scarborough, had been very remote figures who occasionally terrified those who worked below them. He says:

Lord Maclean went out of his way to make everyone feel they were important and the job they were doing was absolutely vital. His friendliness was instant and lasting. On the day we heard of the assassination of Lord Mountbatten, he came into the office and found we were rushed off our feet. Telephones were ringing like mad and secretaries were running about all over the place. The funeral arrangements had to be made in a great hurry. There were simply not enough hands to cope with all the work. Lord Maclean took one look and said, 'Give me something to do – I don't care what it is, let me help.' So we gave him a list of people who had to be telephoned personally and off he went to his office and worked his way down the list making sure that everyone who had to be told was contacted. I cannot imagine either of his two predecessors doing that. He also provided beer and sandwiches – to everyone's surprise.

He immediately set the tone of his term of office on the day he arrived at St James's Palace. The Lord Chamberlain's room is situated on the ground floor in what used to be the dining-room of the Duke of Glouces-ter. The only article belonging to the Duke that remained was the carpet and Sir Eric Penn, as Comptroller, thought it would be a good idea to make the room a little more comfortable by adding a few easy chairs, a sofa, some table lamps and chintz curtains. Chips would have none of it. John Titman says:

He told us to get him some hard wooden chairs and a desk because he didn't want visitors hanging around too long. So out went the easy chairs, the sofa and the soft furnishings and I can never remember going into that room, summer or winter and finding the windows closed. He was a fresh-air fiend no matter what the weather was like.

Another of the Lord Chamberlain's duties is to Chair the Committee that awards the Royal Warrants to tradesmen who have supplied goods or services to a member of the Royal Family for more than three years. The Warrants are highly sought after and add considerable prestige to the companies who are able to display them. In the small town of Ballater near Balmoral, almost every shop has the Royal coat of arms over the doorway, but the right to show they are suppliers to the Royal Family has to be earned, and the Lord Chamberlain's department inves-tigates every applicant thoroughly. John Titman says that Lord Maclean went fully into every individual or firm no matter how large or small. He guarded jealously the Warrants which he was required to sign on behalf of the Queen and the Duke of Edinburgh.

In spite of the fact that Martin Charteris had hoped for a Lord Cham-berlain with political knowledge, Chips himself always felt that the Lord Chamberlain should stay out of political matters. But he did think it was important to be known to leading politicians in order to make himself available should his help be required. For this reason he became a frequent visitor to the House of Lords where he saw it as part of his duty to meet all new peers and introduce himself as the Queen's Lord Chamberlain. He says that one or two were surprised, and later delighted that the Queen's representative should single them out in this manner.

The Lord Chamberlain also became a target for several of the Lords and Ladies of the House when their expected invitations to Palace functions such as Royal Garden Parties hadn't materialised. It sometimes required all his diplomacy and tact to explain that such invitations did not automatically follow year after year.

Every Prime Minister who served the Queen during Lord Maclean's time at St James's Palace found himself invited to dinner or one of the receptions that were held in his private apartments. Some had been friends since before he became Lord Chamberlain, others he was meeting for the first time, as was the case with Harold Wilson (now Lord Wilson of Rievaux). On the first occasion that Prime Minister Wilson turned up he made himself slightly unpopular by tapping out his pipe all over the drawing-room carpet. Mary Wilson apologised on her husband's behalf saying 'don't worry he's always doing it.' Chips replied, 'He may do it at home but not on my carpet.'

Alec Douglas-Home (now Lord Home of the Hirsel) had known Chips for many years before he became Lord Chamberlain and his reaction to his old friend's appointment was: 'Thank goodness there's another Scot in the Household.' Lord Home is another who believes that Chips' greatest attribute is his honesty; 'He is probably the most honest man I have ever met – in some ways perhaps a little too honest. I cannot imagine him telling a lie – even a tiny white one.'

Edward Heath was another visitor to St James's Palace and he was also a guest at the Palace of Holyroodhouse during the week when Chips was acting as Lord High Commissioner of the Church of Scotland. But Chips never found Heath the easiest person to get on with and did not come to regard him as a particularly close friend. Perhaps it was Edward Heath's extreme reservation that made people feel he was cold and unapproachable, but there was one exception and that took place in Edinburgh in May, 1985. One of Lady Maclean's Ladies-in-Waiting had been designated Mr Heath's partner at a dinner party and she was dreading the evening having been warned that he was not the easiest companion. Lord Maclean looked down the table during the evening and was surprised and delighted to find the former Prime Minister in animated conversation with all those around him. The Lady-in-Waiting reported afterwards that Mr Heath had been the most charming companion and her fears were completely unfounded.

The Prime Minister with whom both Lord and Lady Maclean found the easiest rapport was James Callaghan. He and his wife Audrey became frequent guests at St James's Palace in a friendship that far surpassed the normal working relationship between a leading political figure and the Head of the Queen's Household. Elizabeth Maclean and Audrey Callaghan have remained firm friends since their husbands have both left public office, and it's also a fact that Mr and Mrs Callaghan have remained on the Royal guest list. They have been invited to Balmoral for weekends with the Queen and remain on the best of terms with other members of the Royal Family.

Lady Maclean's contribution to the success of her husband's tenure as Lord Chamberlain cannot be overestimated. Every member of the Household the author spoke to mentioned her in almost the same breath as Chips. If he was an expert in 'breaking the ice' with diplomats who were accredited to the Court of St James's, she was equally at home in showing the wives of the Ambassadors and High Commissioners how to settle in to the routine of life in the capital city. Her skill at dealing with ladies who had come from the Third World countries in particular was demonstrated over and over as she took them under her wing and introduced them into the intricacies of Royal protocol and diplomatic behaviour.

If a couple had arrived in London for the first time, the husband usually had the services of his own staff or the Foreign Office to show him the ropes. His wife on many occasions was left to fend for herself. This was where Elizabeth Maclean came into her own. If there was a new arrival on the scene, the Lord Chamberlain's wife would quickly arrange a coffee morning in order that the newcomer could meet as many of her colleagues as possible. And Elizabeth would also take on the role of surrogate 'nanny', going around the shops, arranging sight-seeing trips and organising visits to the theatre, so that the initial loneliness that everyone feels in a new country would be lessened.

It was a role in which she excelled and one she thoroughly enjoyed. A gregarious person herself all her life, having been brought up sur-rounded by family and friends, she is, nevertheless, all too aware of how intimidating life at Court can be.

There is one story told of a weekend party held by the Queen at Sandringham. Her Majesty does not often invite members of her House-hold to join the Royal Family at her private residence, but on this occasion she had asked Lord and Lady Maclean for the weekend. Apparently it was only the presence of Elizabeth that saved the week-end for Chips. As a servant of the Queen he found it difficult to be totally relaxed and to 'let his hair down' in front of the Royal Family, as they all do when they are together. Elizabeth, however, enjoyed Sandringham to the full, with her easy charm and complete lack of self-consciousness, and the occasion turned what could have been an uncomfortable forty-eight hours, into a relaxed, pleasant and normal country-house week-end party.

Lady Susan Hussey has been a Lady-in-Waiting to the Queen for more than twenty years, a fact which is hard to believe when you meet her. She is startlingly good looking, a vivacious brunette and still retains an enormous enthusiasm for her job. But when she first met Chips as Lord Chamberlain she was on her guard. 'I thought he looked a formidable figure', she recalls. 'He was very stern and looked as if there wasn't an ounce of humour in him. I realise now that it was probably because he was rather nervous about taking on the job as Head of the Queen's Household, but at the same time he seemed a bit frightening to me.' For six months Lady Susan did her best not to come into too much contact with Lord Maclean and then one day she found herself sitting next to him at lunch in the Palace:

I had made a slight error that morning. It was nothing much and I can't even remember now what it was all about, but he had noticed and told me off, in a charming old-fashioned way. And then all of a sudden I noticed a twinkle in his eye and he smiled. From that moment I knew it was going to be all right and throughout the thirteen years he was with us all the Ladies-in-Waiting came to regard him with the greatest affection. We could always call on him if we needed help and after every ceremonial occasion he found time to come and talk to us and he was always ready with a word of praise if things had gone particularly well.

Susan Hussey, who is an astute observer of the Royal scene after her many years' experience at close quarters, always felt however that Chips never quite got over the feeling of awe at finding himself as Head of the Household. Where other courtiers could relax in the company of the Queen and the Duke of Edinburgh, Chips always regarded himself as a servant and no more, and he never fully recovered from a sense of wonder at finding himself in this exalted position.

Other members of the Royal Household believe that it was this very feeling which made him such an outstanding success. As someone who had been 'plucked from nowhere' to occupy one of the most prestigous positions in the world, it would have been very easy to have become 'all too aware of one's own position'. It's not unknown for some of those who work in close proximity to the Royal Family to become 'more Royal than the Royals', but this was never the case with Chips Maclean. He never lost sight of the fact that he was a Royal servant in exactly the same way as the man who packs parcels in the basement of Buckingham Palace. It would be ingenuous to suppose that the Head of the Household is regarded in the same way – it simply isn't so. But Chips managed to instil into almost every single member of the Household a feeling of team spirit – of belonging.

John Titman says that in his opinion Lord Maclean was responsible for significant changes within the Household. Prior to his appointment there had been a great dividing line between the various levels of staff. To a large number of people working at lower levels in the palace, the Lord Chamberlain had been as obscure a figure as the Queen herself. Lord Maclean altered all this. His practice of showing himself at regular intervals to every person in every department, and more than this, in actually taking an active interest in what they were doing and remembering them when they next met, was a masterly piece of industrial relations by someone who really did care. John Titman says: 'He was a breath of fresh air who brought a touch of democracy to the Royal Household.'

His colleague and near neighbour Sir Alistair Aird, the Queen Mother's Equerry, says of all the things he will remember about Chips Maclean as Lord Chamberlain one event stands out. Just after a Christmas party at St James's Palace, there was a knock on the door:

We opened the door and standing on the doorstep was Chips dressed as a continental waiter complete with apron and beret with a moustache painted on. He had brought the 'left-overs' from the party and half a bottle of champagne, so in they came.

Not quite the usual picture one imagines of the Queen's Lord Chamberlain perhaps but a useful illustration of the human face of a very public and normally dignified figure.

Perhaps the outstanding occasion in the public's eye will remain the Wedding of the Prince of Wales in July, 1981. It was the biggest media event ever staged, with a worldwide television audience of more than 600 million and while the needs of the radio and television producers were taken into realistic consideration by the man who was responsible for the arrangments, Chips was determined that it was not going to become simply a television spectacular.

He had already helped to write another page in the history of the Royal Family on the morning of Tuesday 24th February. At 11 o'clock an investiture was taking place in Buckingham Palace. Shortly before the Queen began the presentation, Chips announced:

It is with the greatest pleasure that The Queen and The Duke of Edinburgh announce the betrothal of their beloved son The Prince of Wales to the Lady Diana Spencer, daughter of the Earl Spencer and the Honourable Mrs Shand-Kydd.

There was a momentary pause and then, encouraged by the Lord Chamberlain, enthusiastic applause broke out – the first time this had happened at an investiture.

The wedding was not regarded as a State Occasion, which is why, when the Lord Chamberlain preceded the Queen into St Paul's Cathedral he was wearing morning dress, but not carrying his Wand of Office. But it was the most public of private affairs with 2,500 guests in St Paul's. One of the reasons why St Paul's was preferred to Westminster Abbey was that the Abbey can accomodate only 1,800.

Had the wedding been a State Occasion it would have become the responsibility of the Earl Marshall, the Duke of Norfolk who looks after such events as the Coronation, the Investiture of the Prince of Wales or the funeral of the Sovereign.

Jay Cocks writing in *Time* magazine said: 'Like all good extravaganzas the Royal Wedding requires a producer (the Lord Chamberlain) and a director, Col Johnston, who recently received a knighthood for his organisational skills.'

So the two men with the ultimate responsibility of overseeing the marriage of the Heir to the Throne recruited an additional seven people to augment their normal office complement of twelve, and between them these nineteen men and women handled the invitations, the seating arrangements in the cathedral, the route along which the wedding procession would run, the wedding breakfast at Buckingham Palace, the order of the service, accommodation for guests of the Royal Family and a million and one other details necessary to ensure that the wedding proceeded with the same smooth efficiency that characterises all Royal events.

Shortly before the Wedding Day, the Lord Chamberlain and the Crown Equerry set off in the early hours of the morning to check the route from Clarence House to St Paul's Cathedral. Sir John Miller, the Crown Equerry, was experiencing certain problems over Ludgate Hill leading to St Pauls. It's a very steep rise and the horse-drawn carriages could have had difficulty if it had been raining on the day. Eventually Sir John pronounced himself satisfied that every eventuality had been catered for, and that, as usual, things would run like clockwork on the actual day of the wedding.

Then, the evening before the wedding, the Lord Chamberlain received a telephone call from the Crown Equerry to inform him of a very tricky situation. Lady Diana Spencer had decided to use her female prerogative and to arrive at the church two minutes late. Sir John was dismayed. He said, 'I've been in Royal service for twenty-five years and never once have I been asked to arrange a schedule to run late.' It was a dilemma. If the bride's carriage arrived late at St Paul's would the Crown Equerry get the blame? Should he stick to the timetable that had been worked out and published, or should he accede to the request from the future Queen and allow her the privilege every woman is due? There is no record of the advice the Lord Chamberlain gave, but on the day, the bride's carriage arrived at the steps of St Paul's just slightly late – enough to fulfil her wish, but not enough to upset the rest of the programme.

That the wedding went without a hitch is now historical fact and at the end of that memorable day millions of television viewers saw the new Princess of Wales kiss Lord Maclean as she stepped into the train at Waterloo Station on the first leg of her honeymoon journey. It was a delightfully spontaneous gesture of appreciation by the young bride, and one which took him completely by surprise. Afterwards the Lord Chamberlain commented that it was a lovely gesture which he accepted on behalf of all the people who had worked so hard to make the day such an outstanding success, but privately Chips was slightly amazed. Other senior members of the Household were also a little dismayed to see the balloons tied to the coach that carried the Royal couple away from Buckingham Palace – traditions die hard in those who serve the Sovereign!

When the time came for Chips to retire as Lord Chamberlain, the members of his department decided to give him a 'going away' party. John Johnston took over the arrangements. Chips, though secretly pleased that it was taking place, was nevertheless highly embarrassed if he stumbled in on any of the pre-party discussions. As a very private person he finds public demonstrations of emotion embarrassing and he really wanted to know nothing at all about the party until the day.

Then came the moment when he had his final audience of the Queen to take his leave of Her Majesty. Traditionally the retiring Lord Chamberlain offers his Wand of Office back to the Sovereign. The Queen returned it to Chips as a memento of his thirteen years as Head of her Household and asked him if he had ever had occasion to use it. The Wand, though symbolic of course these days, used to be employed to keep unruly members of the Court in order. Chips replied that he nearly had to apply it during one of the Diplomatic Receptions, when one of the guests from an overseas country became a little 'over enthusiastic'. The Queen said that she remembered the occasion and she too had noticed the incident.

Then Her Majesty presented Chips with the Royal Victorian Chain, one of the rarest honours the Sovereign can bestow, and invited him to become her Chief Steward at Hampton Court Palace. What it meant was that instead of having to retire completely from the Royal Household, Chips would be able to 'keep a finger on the pulse' as Her Majesty's representative at what is arguably the most beautiful of all Royal palaces. The duties are not too arduous, indeed are very pleasant. Whenever there is a major function at which members of the Royal Family are going to be present, the Chief Steward welcomes them to Hampton

One of the early spectaculars stage-managed by the Lord Chamberlain was the wedding of Princess Anne and Captain Mark Phillips in November, 1973. Westminster Abbey was the setting and the event was seen by 500 million people throughout the world, live on television.

One of the happiest of Royal occasions as Lord Maclean, the Lord Chamberlain, shakes hands with King Carl XVI Gustaf of Sweden at a Nobel Prize reception in December, 1982. In the foreground, Queen Silvia is obviously delighted at something that's been said.

The funeral of the Duke of Windsor, who died in May, 1972, was one of the most delicate situations the Lord Chamberlain had to deal with. The Duchess had never been allowed to use the title 'Royal Highness' and Chips needed all his diplomatic skills as he escorted her to the aircraft taking her back to her home in Paris.

'Catching a crab' – once a year the Lord Chamberlain accompanies the Turk family (for generations Keepers of the Queen's Swans), as they patrol the upper reaches of the Thames for the ceremony of 'Swan-Upping'. As a former 'wet-bob', he should have known better than to try to keep up with these hardy rivermen.

The Lord Chamberlain bids farewell on behalf of the Queen to Princess Anne and Captain Mark Phillips as they leave London *en route* to join *Britannia* for their honeymoon cruise.

Elizabeth Maclean continues to knit quietly in spite of the attentions of Master Peter Phillips, the Queen's first grandchild, on board *Britannia* as they cruise around the coast of Scotland in the summer sunshine – August, 1983.

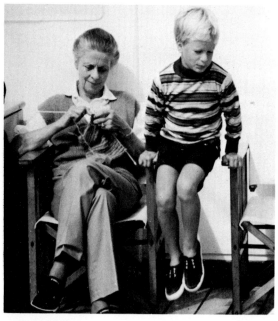

Whenever the Queen returns from overseas, she is greeted by her Lord Chamberlain. Here Chips follows Her Majesty ashore from the Royal Yacht, after welcoming her back from another of her trips abroad.

When Chips retired as Lord Chamberlain, the Queen and Prince Philip presented him with this magnificent pair of glass decanters. And in a delightful gesture which showed just how aware they were of Elizabeth's contribution, they included her name in the inscription.

Shortly after his retirement as Lord Chamberlain, Chips was appointed by the Queen to be Chief Steward of Hampton Court Palace. Here, the Queen, accompanied by her Chief Steward, inspects some of the millions of pounds worth of damage caused by a fire at Hampton Court Palace in March, 1986.

'A thrill for Emma' – Chips' elder granddaughter is presented to the Queen at Dalmahoy near Edinburgh, where Her Majesty had come to watch the Duke of Edinburgh taking part in a carriage driving contest. Looking on is the Crown Equerry Lt. Col. Sir John Miller.

The Macleans' daughter, Janet, at home in Norfolk with her husband Nicholas Barne, another Scots Guardsman – and their two sons, Hamish and Alistair.

Chips' and Elizabeth's first grandchild – Emma – Lachlan and Mary Maclean's daughter, already showing the promise of the beauty to come as she is photographed in the Scottish Highlands.

Three of Lachlan's children, Andrew, Alexandra and Malcolm, photographed on one of the ancient cannon at Duart, summer 1985. Malcolm was the third generation of the Macleans to enter Royal service when he was appointed a Page of Honour to the Queen at the State Opening of Parliament in November 1985.

Duart Castle from the sea – it has lasted seven hundred years and who is to say it won't last another seven hundred?

Court and remains in attendance. Along with the position goes the tenancy of one of the nicest of all the Grace-and-Favour homes, Wilderness House, alongside the famous Maze. The house was once lived in by Capability Brown while designing the Royal gardens and Elizabeth Maclean has quickly established her own personality in the colour schemes and furnishings. One advantage that Wilderness House has over the apartment in St James's Palace, is an ultra-modern kitchen where Elizabeth can demonstrate her remarkable culinary expertise. Fortunate visitors are frequently sent away with one of her special loaves of soda bread if they are lucky, and nobody ever has cause to complain about the standard of food served at the Macleans' table.

In the dining-room are two magnificent crystal decanters, presented to the Lord Chamberlain on his retirement by the Queen and the Duke of Edinburgh. On one is engraved a likeness of Duart Castle from a photograph taken by Prince Andrew, and on the other the words: 'To Chips and Elizabeth from Elizabeth and Philip', a charming reminder that the Queen and her husband fully realised the part played by Lady Maclean during the time Chips was Head of the Household.

A serious fire at Hampton Court Palace in March 1986 caused millions of pounds of damage and the death of an elderly resident in one of the Grace-and-Favour apartments. Fortunately, most of the treasures had been removed for cleaning.

Shortly after Chips retired, Queen Elizabeth, the Queen Mother decided to give a luncheon party in his honour and she paid him the compliment of asking him if there were any special guests he would like invited. There cannot be many people who can claim such a unique going-away present!

When Chips looks back on his thirteen years as Lord Chamberlain, meeting Presidents and Prime Ministers, Kings, Queens and Princes; attending the most important events in the Royal Calendar as a major participant, and witnessing at first-hand the behaviour of the most powerful people in the world, what is the one memory that remains uppermost in his heart?

To find out it's necessary to go back to the earliest days of his time in Royal service. It was the first State Banquet at Buckingham Palace to be organised by the incoming Lord Chamberlain, when for the first of many times, he would be required to walk backwards across that seemingly never-ending carpet. A very nervous Chips had performed his duties impeccably and he was standing at the entrance to the Music Room as the Royal Party left after the meal. As Queen Elizabeth, the Queen Mother passed the Lord Chamberlain she paused for an instant, glanced at Chips and said, 'Well done!' Just two words which he will always remember.

Chapter 8

CLAN MACLEAN

Charles Hector Fitzroy Maclean is a Privy Councillor, Knight of the Thistle, Knight Grand Cross of the Royal Victorian Order, the 11th Baronet, a Life Peer and 27th Chief of the Clan Maclean. There are those of his countrymen who suggest that his 'Kt' is more prestigious than any of his other honours and there are those of his clan who would claim that his Chiefship is by far the most important of his titles and responsibilities.

In this chapter it is the author's intention to try and trace briefly the history of the Clan Maclean, or rather that line from which Maclean of Duart is descended. It is not intended to be the definitive version; there is simply not enough time and space to do that here, and in any case, others, more qualified, have chronicled the exploits and achievements of the Macleans overall elsewhere.

So in looking at the Macleans of Duart, I offer my apologies to those branches of the Clan who hail from Ardgour, Borreray, Blaich, Lochbuie, Drimnacross, Drimmin, Pennycross and Kinlochaline; not to mention those from Sweden, Japan and the Netherlands. Each one is deserving of a story of his own, but I trust each will find something of interest in the Macleans of Duart, from where the Chiefs of the Clan originate.

The Highland Clan system continued virtually unchanged for nearly six centuries. There was only one fundamental qualification for membership and that was by right of blood. Each member of a Highland clan bore the same surname and was in some respect related to all the other members of the clan, and each was descended from the same stock. At the head of the clan was the Chief, the ultimate power and authority. Immediately below him were the Chieftains, many of whom founded their own branches or septs of the clan which were autonomous in most things, but each owed his final allegiance to the Chief and would respond to the call to arms whenever it came.

Throughout the clans of Scotland there was a remarkable democracy, not encountered in any other feudal system. Although the Chief was the sole and undisputed leader, his clansmen regarded themselves as his equal in terms of dignity and standing, and the success of the clan depended to a great extent on mutual respect.

The normal line of succession was from father to son, or failing that, to the nearest male relative. But there was also an ancient Scottish law called tanistry which allowed a Chief to name his successor and a further law which permitted nine elders of the clan to petition the Crown for recognition of a suitable candidate if the direct line of descent had died out. This has never happened in Clan Maclean.

Charles Maclean is able to trace his ancestry in direct line back to the 13th century when the first chief was Gillean of the Battleaxe – Gillean being the name from which the Macleans take their name and from whom they trace their origin as a clan. Gillean became Chief somewhere in the middle of the 13th century – the actual date is unknown, but historians are generally agreed that he was at his peak around the year 1250, when he controlled large areas in the north of Mull. Mull has always been the home of the Macleans and it was here that the Clan originated. It was Gillean who chose Duart as the site on which was built the castle which was to remain the focal point for the clan for seven centuries.

He was a fearsome warrior, but in spite of his warlike soubriquet – which was actually earned not only because he used the axe as a weapon in battle, but also because his followers saw it embedded in a tree and so found him when he became lost on a hunting expedition – he was in fact a man who believed he was above all else, free and was determined to be subservient to no one. The very essence of Highland life at the time was freedom; to hold what was one's own against allcomers. It was while Gillean was Chief of the Clan that the foundations of Duart Castle were laid although the precise date of the start of the building of the fortress is lost in the mists of time.

When Gillean died, having laid the foundations of the great Clan, he was succeeded by one of his three sons, Gille-Iosa of Macgillean. Like his father before him, he was a great warrior who distinguished himself on the battlefield as a supporter of Alexander III of Scotland. His name means 'servant of Jesus' and his part in the battle that took place on the Ayrshire coast on 2nd October, 1263 between the Scottish monarch and the Norwegians under King Haco, earned him an honourable mention in the history of the times. Gille-Iosa died in 1300 and his son Malcolm became third Chief of the Clan Maclean – so within the short space of half a century a dynasty had been established which was to last until the present day.

By now the Macleans possessed a great deal of land on the Island of Mull and when Malcolm died in the reign of King David Bruce, his son John inherited vast areas surrounding Duart as far south as Lochbuie. The fourth chief was known as Ian Dubh or Black John and little is known of his reign apart from the fact that the Chiefs of the clans depended on the patronage of the Lords of the Isles who maintained their feudal superiority, with a ruthlessness tempered only slightly with patrician benevolence.

By this period, the mid-14th century, the Macleans, although living at Duart, had not yet been granted legal title to the castle and surrounding land. But when Black John died in the reign of Robert II, his son Lachlan Lubanach, who succeeded him as Chief, took appropriate steps to ensure that Duart would become the legal property of the Macleans in perpetuity. He did this by applying to Donald, Second Lord of the Isles, for a charter in 1390, and in that year, on 12th July, at Ardtonish, the 'custody and constableship of the Castle of Duard' was granted to Lachlan Maclean and Duart (as it is spelt today) became the legal and undisputed home of the Chiefs of the Clan Maclean.

A hundred years later the charter was confirmed in the High Court at Glasgow. And so Lachlan, the fifth Chief of the Clan was the man responsible for making Duart the legal property of the Clan and as such he is generally regarded as the first Maclean of Duart, but there is no doubt that the castle, or at the very least its site, had been occupied by the Macleans for more than a hundred years before. Lachlan was succeeded by his son Hector, known as Red Hector of the Battles. If the Macleans as a Clan had the reputation as being the finest swordsmen in Scotland, their sixth Chief distinguished himself as their leader by meeting and defeating all challengers. He was a fearless fighter whose greatest triumph was to command a fleet of ships against the English off the Irish coast, when he not only defeated the numerically superior ships but landed in Ireland and attacked the city of Dublin itself.

Hector's son Lachlan Bronnach became seventh Chief of the Macleans. He was a man of great girth as befits someone called Bronnach (fat-bellied) and perhaps it was because of his enormous stomach and the effort required to carry it around, that he did not inherit the warlike tendencies of his famous warrior father. It wasn't until 1427 that Lachlan Bronnach began to earn his place in the history of the clan, when, as a supporter of Alexander, Third Lord of the Isles, he was taken prisoner by King James I and incarcerated in Tantallon Castle after a battle at Inverness. Upon his release he began to exhibit the characteristics of his forebears and became a warrior who enthusiastically led his men in attacks upon his neighbours, and indeed any who opposed him.

Lachlan Bronnach married twice and had four sons. The first, Donald, was illegitimate and was born to a daughter of Maclean of Kingerloch and from whom the families of Ardgour and Borreray are descended. His heir, Lachlan Og, was by his first wife, Margaret, daughter of the Earl of Mar. When she died, he married Fionnaghal, the daughter of William Macleod of Harris, by whom he had two further sons, Neil of

Ross and John Garbh of Coll.

Donald Maclean realised that he would have no inheritance from his father and he determined to make his own fortune. As right of conquest was the only alternative, he armed a number of followers with the consent of his father, and attacked the McMaster Clan at Ardgour. To carry out such an attack on a neighbouring Chieftain would have needed the consent, if not the support of the Lord of the Isles. This must have been forthcoming, because McMaster received no help from his Lord, and when he and his son had been killed by Maclean, his lands were immediately and legally transferred to the young Maclean in a charter which was later confirmed by King James I.

Lachlan Bronnach's second legal son, Neil of Ross, was an unusual son of a Highland Chief in that he displayed little aptitude for battle and waging war on his neighbours. He was given possession of Lehire in the Isle of Mull by his father, and his branch of the family retained it until his own grandson was killed and the estates forfeited.

Neil's brother John Garbh inherited more of the Maclean's warlike tendencies and he was similar in his attitude to his illegitimate brother Donald, in that he was determined to acquire lands of his own by whatever means he could. After being given the Island of Coll by the Lord of the Isles, he also managed to obtain possession of Rhum, claiming he had bought it from the owner. This was disputed and John Garbh captured the unfortunate man and kept him prisoner for nine months, after which, not surprisingly, the 'sale' was agreed.

Meanwhile, Lachlan Og took command of the Clan in the latter part of the 15th century, a time of great change throughout Scotland and more particularly in the Western Isles. In the same way that the Clansmen were loyal to their Chief above all others, so too the Chiefs were loyal to the Lords of the Isles and regarded them as the ultimate authority, even more so than the Sovereign, who was in many cases a distant and remote figure.

It says a great deal for the statesman-like attitude of Lachlan Og that he managed to keep his holdings and his Clan intact throughout the years of internecine warfare involving his feudal superiors and the King's forces. He was a man of great political acumen whose negotiating skill saved him even from the machinations of his father-in-law, the first Earl of Argyll, who attempted to brand him with the same treason he had accused the Lord of the Isles of displaying.

His wife Catherine, provided him with an heir, Hector and two daughters, Fionnaghal and Anne, both of whom made successful marriages and brought extra land into the family.

The exact date of the death of Lachlan Og is unknown, but records show that he certainly lived until 1463. His son became known as Hector the Swarthy, a man of natural violence who entered into the spirit of Chiefship with an enthusiasm that included using as his personal weapon a battle-axe of the same sort favoured by his ancestor Gillean. Hector was loyal to the Lord of the Isles and fought many battles on his side against those who would usurp his power, including at one time his own illegitimate son. Throughout his lifetime Hector was involved in battles all over the Western Isles before he died in 1500. Some records show that he was in fact alive much later than this, and there are claims that he was killed in 1513 at the Battle of Flodden Field. However, this has not been proved and seems highly unlikely, in that, had Hector fought at Flodden Field, he would have been well into his nineties, and hardy though the Highlanders were in those days, a nonogenarian leading his clan into battle would almost certainly have received some recognition, so this colourful but untrue story must go down as yet another legend of the Highlands.

There *was* a Maclean who fell at Flodden Field, but this was more probably Hector's illegitimate son, Lachlan, who is acknowledged by Scottish historians as the 10th Chief of the Macleans. Little is known of the period of his Chieftainship mainly because he was the first leader of the Macleans to be born illegitimate. But his father's marriage had produced no other children so there was no challenge to the succession.

If accounts of the great battle at Flodden Field are to be believed, Lachlan died in an heroic manner, shielding King James IV from arrows of the English archers who surrounded him. The same accounts state that by the time he was killed there was a solid wall around him, composed entirely of the bodies of his Clansmen. Lachlan had married and produced a legal heir and successor who became 11th Chief on the death of his father. Lachlan Catanach, a word which means either rough or shaggy. He adopted the latter description and was known as Lachlan the Shaggy.

At the time he inherited his title, the Macleans were the most power-ful Clan in the Western Isles. The Lords of the Isles, the traditional overlords, had had their power depleted to a large extent and the clans which had previously owed them allegiance, were now in the main, independent, although the Macleans together with other clans of equal status, remained friendly with the Lords of the Isles and supported them in their arguments with the Earls of Argyll.

One result of the defeat at Flodden Field was the immediate plotting for power among the various factions who had survived. Lachlan the Shaggy was a prime mover in the rebellion which broke out to restore the Macdonalds to the Lordship of the Isles. The Macleans became involved in a number of battles, with Lachlan Catanach assisted by his kinsmen from Lochbuie and Ardgour, against their traditional enemies the Campbells. But if Lachlan Catanach was a brave warrior, he was also a simple soul who was easily deceived and frequently he found himself fighting on the wrong side because of lies he had been told by those he thought were his friends.

He was also impetuous to a degree. One of the famous legends which has grown up around his lifetime concerns the story of 'The Lady's Rock'. The accuracy of the story is open to conjecture, but it is certainly entertaining and bears retelling. Lachlan's first marriage was to Elizabeth, daughter of Archibald Campbell, the second Earl of Argyll. She had been unable to provide him with a son and heir and there are stories that she also tried on several occasions to murder her husband. He decided to get rid of her in a unique and picturesque fashion. He took her out to a flat rock which lies between the Isle of Lismore and the coast of Mull and abandoned her, after making sure she was properly bound and gagged. The rock is completely submerged at high tide and Lachlan, so the legend has it, was relying on the water to solve his problem. Unfortunately for him, but happily for his wife, a boat passed by rowed by two kinsmen of the intended victim's brother. They rescued her and returned her to the safety of the Earl of Argyll's custody.

The Campbells contained their resentment for many years, but in 1527, Lachlan, who had by now made his peace with the King and been assured of safe passage, went to Edinburgh on business. He was asleep in bed when Sir John Calder, brother of the Earl of Argyll crept into the room and stabbed him to death.

Between the episode of 'The Lady's Rock' and his death in 1527 Lachlan Catanach had married on two more occasions. The first was to Margaret, daughter of another branch of the Campbells, Sir Dugald, by whom he had no children, and so that marriage too was short-lived, and he then married Marian Maclean of Treshnish who was more successful in providing him with the sons he wanted. There were two: Hector Mor who became his heir and Ailean who was to achieve a fearsome reputation as a notorious pirate. There was also an illegitimate son Patrick, who subsequently became Bishop of the Isles.

The 12th Chief of the Macleans, Hector Mor earned the name Hector the Great during the forty-one years he led the Clan. It was during his period that Duart Castle was turned from a fortress used solely as a resting place for the warriors and fighting men of the Clan, into the comparatively comfortable home it was subsequently to become. Hector Mor was a patrician figure whose method of leadership was closer to that of more recent times than was usual in the 16th century. Although he resisted any attempts by his warlike neighbours to impinge upon his kindgom, the official Scottish archives refer to him as being 'good, kind, affectionate and brave, an accomplished politician . . . and that in him the clan realized all it desired in a noble chieftain.'

He was responsible for building the Great Tower of Duart and for providing comfortable, if modest, homes for his followers. His influence was recognised by many of the most powerful people in the land and he sat in Parliament acting as counsel to the King. The estate prospered under his direction and his daughters all made successful marriages to influential Scottish families. On one occasion when the fourth Earl of Argyll had assembled a larger force to invade Mull, it was brought to his attention that Maclean was more than ready to meet him 'either in peace or otherwise'. It was suggested that a much more satisfactory method of consolidation would be for the Earl to marry one of Hector's beautiful daughters and for his own daughter, Janet, to marry Hector's son and heir, Eachann Og. This was agreed to and the double marriage took place at Duart thereby binding both families in a relationship neither had thought possible. But these marriages of convenience did little in the long term to heal the breach between the Campbells and the Macleans.

However, that they were successful in allowing Maclean to extend the holdings and influence of his family is demonstrated by the following extracts from official records of the period:

On January 9, 1539-40, Hector passes over a charter in favour of his son and heir the lands of Torosay, castle of Duard, Lands of Brolass, Tiree, with office of baillery thereof, lands in Knapdale, Jura, Morvern, and Lochaber, but reserving life rent for same. November 12, 1542 he received a charter for lands of Kilmichell and More in Islay.

4th February 1548-9. Precept for charter under the great seal, to Hector McClane of Doward, heritably, of the lands and barony of Argour, which belonged before to John McCarlych of Argour, but now to the Queen as ultima haeres, because the said John died without lawful heirs; to hold of the crown on the same terms as Doward, being included therein.

23 June, 1553, he received charter for the lands of Ulva and Laganvalsagary, in the shire of Terbert.

26th January, 1557, he gave a charter to Janet Campbell, daughter of the Earl of Argyle, of the lands of Dunnowlycht, Rannochquhen, etc., in Knapdale and Lochaber.

Hector Mor had married a daughter of Alexander MacDonald of Islay at an early age and she provided him with nine children – two sons and seven daughters. His eldest son was the aforementioned Eachann Og, who was to marry Janet, daughter of the Earl of Argyll, and who was to succeed his father as Chief. The second son was John Dubh who was to become the founder of the Maclean sept at Kinlochaline. Of the seven daughters, two were named Catherine; the first unmarried and the second, who was considered to be the most beautiful of all his children, became an important part of his plan to consolidate relationships with the Campbells when she was married to Archibald, fourth Earl of Argyll.

Hector's brother, Ailean was known as Allan o' the Wisp because of his disturbing habit of setting fire to buildings with straw. He became a notorious and successful pirate because according to feudal laws he did not inherit any of his father's estates as a second son. And like others before him, he set out to secure his own fortune in the best way he was able. He lent his talents to whoever was the best paymaster, even occasionally against his brother Hector Mor, but more often on his side. And in spite of his frequent brushes with death he died peacefully in bed in 1551.

One of the most repeated, and perhaps apocrypyhal stories about him concerns his attempts to secure the hand of the beautiful daughter of one of his neighbours. She did not return his love and he, infuriated by the rebuff, determined to repay the insult to his manhood. He forced her to the edge of a steep cliff intending to throw her over, but a servant saw what was happening and caught hold of Ailean pushing him over the edge. Ailean was lucky enough to land on a ledge some way down the cliff and there he remained until he had begged the lady's forgiveness and promised no revenge on the servant. He was then rescued and this incident gave rise to the saying 'to be left on the shelf'. It was also from this moment that Ailean turned to crime as a career, and as a footnote it is interesting to observe that he never married once his original proposal had been rejected.

Hector Mor was considered to be one of the finest Chiefs the Macleans have ever had and under his leadership the Clan became one of the most powerful and influential in Scotland. He died about the year 1568 to be succeeded by his son Hector the Younger. The 13th Chief inherited great wealth and vast estates from his father, but none of his wisdom or powers of leadership. Within five years he had not only spent all his inheritance, but had plunged the family into great debt. Hector the Younger died in 1573 to be succeeded by his son Lachlan Mor, later to become Sir Lachlan Maclean, though how and when he was created a knight is not clear; the first official reference to a title and baronetcy does not appear until nearly sixty years later. He was called 'Big Lachlan' both because of his physical attributes and his breadth of vision. He had been educated in Edinburgh and spent much of his youth at the Court of King James in Holyrood House where he became a great favourite. After completing his education he returned to Mull to claim his rightful place as Chief of the Macleans and take possession of Duart Castle. He occupied a premier position as head of the most powerful Clan in the Western Isles and his prowess on the battlefield earned him a fearsome reputation. Sir Lachlan also occupies a unique role in the history of the Macleans by becoming the first Chief to reject the Catholic religion and embrace the principles of the Reformation, thereby becoming the first Protestant of his family.

He died on 5th August, 1598 in a clan battle with his old adversaries the Macdonalds on the Isle of Islay, but the method of his death was in contrast to the open, brave manner of his living. A servant who had been rejected by Maclean as unworthy to fight alongside him in battle, had joined the other side. He had obtained a gun and, seeing Sir Lachlan in a vulnerable position, shot him down from a sniper's hide. It was a sad and inauspicious end to a valiant lifetime which was then in its prime. Sir Lachlan was forty-one at the time.

His death brought Eachann Ogg or Young Hector to the leadership of the clan as 15th Chief. He had been trained from an early age to take over from his father and his first task as Chief was to avenge the cowardly murder.

The Macleans and the Macdonalds had fought each other for generations and this final battle was to be the most bloody. The Macleans and their supporters invaded Islay where the Macdonalds fought ferociously to hold what was theirs. But the rage of the Macleans forced the Macdonalds to retreat eventually with hundreds dead and wounded, and the victors took a terrible revenge on the people of Islay. Every building was burned to the ground and every man, woman or child who could be found was killed. However it seems that the blood-letting drained both the Macdonalds and the Macleans of any further wish to fight, and since that date the two families have remained on the best of terms.

Eachann Og was married twice. His first wife gave him his heir, Hector Mor, and his second Isabella, provided a son, Donald who was the predecessor of the Macleans of Sweden.

Eachann Og was thirty-nine when he died in 1618 and his son Big Hector became 16th Chief. In spite of his size and ancestry, Big Hector was a peaceful man by all accounts who inherited a secure and powerful Clan which was not in danger of being over-run or depleted by outside interests. He did not do a great deal to expand his estates, preferring to live at Duart and enjoy the comparative security of his island stronghold during the ten years he was Chief. He married a daughter of Macleod but they had no children and so when he died in 1628 the direct line of succession which had followed from generation to generation since the Clan was founded 400 years earlier, came to an end. The new Chief, the 17th, was Hector's brother Sir Lachlan MacLean, who was also the first baronet. This occurred in 1631 during his first visit to the Court of Charles I, following the death of his brother. The King created him a Baronet of Nova Scotia, with the title of Sir Lachlan MacLean of Morvern. The baronetcy is recorded in the General Register and dated 3rd September, 1631.

The Macleans remained loyal to the King throughout his lifetime, in spite of the attempts of the eighth Earl of Argyll to inveigle them into plots and counter plots. Argyll had first supported the King, Charles I, and then turned on him – and eventually became an ardent admirer and loyal subject of his son Charles II. But long before that the Macleans had fought for His Majesty Charles I under the Marquis of Montrose against the Argylls at Inverlochy on 2nd February, 1645. When the Macleans eventually returned to their homes on Mull they were attacked by a large force of men under the command of the Earl of Argyll. The Chief of the Macleans had ordered his followers not to resist, thinking that in this way the invaders would have no reason to harm them. He was wrong. Practically the whole island was devastated and there were fears at one time that the entire Clan was to be destroyed. Realising the futility of further resistance within the castle, Sir Lachlan made the best terms he could.

With the execution of the King, the Earl of Argyll purchased a number of debts accrued by Sir Lachlan amounting to £30,000. These he used as a means of having the Chief imprisoned for a year. Lachlan was so weakened by his treatment in prison that his supporters prevailed upon him to sign a bond admitting the debt. This he eventually did and he was able to return to Duart, where he died shortly afterwards, on the 18th April, 1648.

His successor was the elder of his two sons, Eachann Ruadh, or Red Hector. He was another in the long line of brave warriors whose courage was matched by his sense of honour. He freely acknowledged the debt his father had passed on to him and made several attempts to pay the Earl of Argyll what was due to him. There is evidence of a single payment of £10,000, a third of the total amount, being paid in one instalment, but because of some confusion over the receipt, this money was never credited to the Maclean account and in later years the total amount of £30,000 still remained.

Red Hector was also a fervent supporter of the Stuart cause. When Charles I was executed in 1649, his son was proclaimed King of Scotland in Edinburgh the following year, and Hector rallied the Maclean Clan to the Royalist banner.

His most notable exploits took place on the battlefield at Inverkeithing against the numerically superior and more experienced soldiers of Cromwell's republican army. On that day, 800 Macleans fought alongside their Chief; only forty survived the battle. Red Hector was killed by a musket shot and he fell, claymore in hand, his body covered in wounds. He was only twenty-seven when he died, but his name had been added to the Maclean role of honour where it still occupies a unique place of distinction.

Red Hector had never married and so for the second time the direct line of succession was interrupted. He had a younger brother Allan, who was only six years old at the time of the Battle of Inverkeithing so his estates were managed by two uncles until he reached manhood. They managed to pay off part of the huge debt to the Argylls, but the matter dragged on year after year without resolve. Even after Charles II was restored to the Monarchy and indicated that he favoured a settlement that would be fair to both parties, the Earl of Argyll managed to delay events sufficiently for his legal advisors to boost the sum owed, from the original £30,000, to the astronomical figure of £120,000 with interest payments.

Sir Allan Maclean seems to have spent most of his Chieftainship pursuing the means of clearing the debt which hung over the Maclean family like a 'sword of Damocles', but without success. He agreed to pay the rents of the Maclean estates directly to the Earl of Argyll until the debt was cleared but the interest payments were so iniquitous that the agreement Allan Maclean signed in good faith, meant that there was virtually no prospect of ever clearing the debt fully.

Like his brother before him, Sir Allan was only twenty-seven when he died and the son he left to succeed him as 20th Chief of the Clan was a mere four years old, so again two relatives were appointed to supervise the estates until he reached his majority. By this time the Clan was determined that the debt to the Campbells should be settled one way or another. If a full accounting of the amounts paid was not agreed to by Argyll, they decided that the only solution was for the Macleans to resort to the sword, and protect what was theirs.

But the casualties suffered at Inverkeithing had sadly depleted the fighting forces of the Macleans and they were not fully prepared for a major encounter. The Earl of Argyll landed on Mull with more than 5,000 men and routed the Macleans. The young Chief, John, was taken from the island for his own safety and Duart was occupied by the invading army.

A garrison was left in charge of the castle and the tenants of the estates were informed that in future their rents were to be paid directly to the Earl of Argyll. At the time the rents became due not a penny was handed over; Argyll obtained an official order from the Edinburgh privy council to carry 'fire and sword' into the Maclean district.

Meanwhile the Chief of the Clan Macdonald who had always been firm friends and supporters of the Macleans, travelled to London to plead the case for the Macleans before the King. It was eventually decided that a public hearing would be held in Edinburgh when for the first time the details of the debt would be brought into the open.

J P Maclean in his *History of the Macleans* published in 1889 gives details of the amount of money that had changed hands and the way in which the original debt had been escalated.

It had started when Sir Lachlan Maclean, the 17th Chief, borrowed money, the exact amount has never been agreed, to finance an army to fight the King in the Civil War. The Earl of Argyll bought up the debts, again for a sum which has not been disclosed and obtained a bond for £30,000. It is commonly believed that the Argylls had not paid more than £10,000 for the debts and this amount was paid, as previously mentioned, by Sir Hector Maclean shortly before the Battle of Inverkeithing.

There was a dispute over whether this money had been credited against the debt, and further amounts of £22,000 were paid between 1652 and 1659. With the subsequent agreements signed by Sir Allan Maclean, and the rents which were paid directly to the Earl of Argyll, by the year 1676, some £100,000 had been paid in total. But because of the delaying tactics employed by the Argylls and their advisers, most of the original debt remained unpaid, and in fact had swollen to around £200,000 by the time the case had been brought before Council in Edinburgh.

The matter was prolonged until 1680, when the King finally decided that enough was enough and issued instructions that the matter was to be resolved once and for all. The Scottish Council was ordered to find that the Earl of Argyll was to be given the Island of Tiree in full settlement of the debt; and so after many years of penury, the Clan Maclean was finally free of its debt to the Earls of Argyll. Maclean was glad to settle the debt and indeed there was a happy outcome two years later, when Argyll had been beheaded for treason, and his estates forfeited. Tiree was restored to Maclean. All this had taken place while the Chief was still too young to control his own affairs and when his guardians died between the years 1868 and 1887 he was old enough to take over the business of the Clan in the knowledge that at last the slate was clean!

So, freed from the need to continually protect his lands from his traditional enemy, John Maclean was able to lead his Clan in the causes they supported at the time. The Highland Clans led by Viscount Dundee were in favour of restoring the monarchy of James II, who had retired to France after his policies had resulted in his dethronement, and the subsequent accession of William and Mary. The most historic battle involving Sir John Maclean and his Clan was undoubtedly that at the Pass of Killicrankie in July, 1689. Sir John leading 500 of his Clansmen was instrumental in winning a significant victory over an enemy many times greater in numbers, but the battle had cost the life of Lord Dundee. His successor proved to be unequal to the task and led his men into a series of defeats, each one depleting their numbers until there were very few of them left to fight.

Meanwhile the 10th Earl of Argyll, anxious to resume hostilities against the Macleans, had petitioned King William to provide him with a commission of 'fire and sword' with which to attack Duart Castle, claiming that Sir John Maclean, by his actions on the side of the Earl of Dundee, had proved himself and his Clan to be enemies of the State. The Commission was granted and Argyll landed on Mull with a force of 2,500 men. Sir John realised that resistance was futile – his small army of immediate Clansmen being the only support he could call on – and fearing that if he did resist the remainder of his Clan would be slaughtered, he surrendered Duart Castle on 31st March, 1692.

He was granted safe passage to London to plead his case before the King who offered him command of a regiment; an offer he declined. After returning to Scotland to settle his private affairs he left for exile in France where, due to a conflict in the stories he was told, he believed that James II was to be restored to the Throne and he attached himself to the Court of the dethroned monarch, where he remained until the accession of Queen Anne in 1702.

A general amnesty was granted to supporters of James and Sir John, believing it included himself, left for London where he was arrested and sent to the Tower until his trial. However he was acquitted and the Queen also gave him a pension of £500 a year for life, which he accepted with gratitude. His courage, which was unquestioned since Killicrankie, was still never in doubt but he spent a great part of the remainder of his life in London with only occasional visits to Scotland. Then in November, 1715 he raised a regiment to fight under the Earl of Mar for the Jacobite cause and the restoration of James III. The opposing armies were needless to say under the command of the age-old enemy of the Macleans, the Earl of Argyll. A decisive battle was fought at Sherrifmuir with 800 Macleans charging behind their Chief. Casualties were about equal on both sides and equally Argyll and Mar claimed victory. Ultimately it was to be the Earl of Argyll who came out on top, as the Earl of Mar's army disbanded shortly afterwards. Sir John was offered passage to France, but he refused, knowing that if he left Scotland again he would be unlikely to return. He had no doubt become dispirited by the forfeiture of his estates and the constant refusal of the Queen to restore them. His health had deteriorated during the months following the battle at Sherrifmuir and he contracted consumption. So with his powers of resistance at their lowest ebb, he died at Gorden Castle, Perth on 12th March, 1716, and an era lasting nearly 450 years had come to an end.

Sir John Maclean would be the last of the powerful and influential Chiefs in the truest sense of the words. No longer would the Macleans be asked to lend their support to the Stuart or any other cause. They were no longer masters of Duart and the Clans were being disarmed. For nearly two centuries succeeding Chiefs would be exiles, born abroad and for the most part spending their lives in foreign parts. Sir John had married only once and his wife, Mary, had provided him with six children, a son named Hector who was to assume the hollow mantle of Chiefstainship, and five daughters. The 21st Chief, Sir Hector Maclean, had been born out of Scotland during his father's exile in France. The birth was recorded in Calais on 6th November, 1703. In 1707 he was brought to England and from there to Scotland where he was left in the care of Donald Maclean on the Island of Coll, with whose family he remained until he was eighteen.

Sir Hector was a scholar who studied at Edinburgh University where he excelled in philosophy, mathematics and civil law. He had been brought up speaking French as a first language, then English and finally Gaelic to a limited extent. In 1721 he returned to France to complete his education and apart from occasional visits to Scotland, he remained in the country of his birth until shortly before the outbreak of the second Jacobite revolution in Scotland in 1745.

On hearing that Bonnie Prince Charlie was raising an army intent on restoring him to the throne, Sir Hector left France and sailed to Edinburgh to fight alongside the Prince. But before he was able to meet up with the Stuart forces he was arrested and sent in chains to London where he remained in prison for two years, before being released under an Act of Grace.

The Maclean Clan had rallied to the Young Pretender even without their Chief, when 500 men led by Charles Maclean of Drimmin, fought what they must have known was going to be their last battle, at Culloden, under the overall command of the Duke of Perth. For the Macleans of Duart it was as if they realised they had little to lose. Their Chief was captured, the castle was in the hands of the enemy and the once all-powerful Clan had been deprived of all infuence and prosperity. So here perhaps was the final and glorious way to end matters one way or another. Either they would win and the new King would restore their former glory, or at worst they would go down fighting in the splendid tradition of centuries of Macleans before them.

History has recorded that the Highlanders fought bravely against overwhelming odds; less than 4,000 Scots against 9,000 highly trained and disciplined troops of the English army. But the outcome was inevitable and bloody. Most of the Macleans were killed and, along with the MacLauchlans and Macgillivrays, they are buried in one very long grave, fifty-six feet long, on the field of Culloden where the mass grave is marked with a memorial tombstone which can still be seen.

Sir Hector, who of course was French by birth, was eventually released from prison as a French prisoner in 1747, remaining abroad for the rest of his life. He died in 1750 during a visit to Rome, a Chief in name only, but one who was still regarded as the head of the family by all Macleans who had stayed in Scotland or been forced to live in other parts of the world.

As far as the Clan system of the Highlands was concerned it meant the end of a lifestyle that had lasted for more than four centuries. Apart from the disarming of the Clans, the British Parliament passed an act that prohibited the wearing of Highland dress on any occasion. This included the kilt and any form of tartan or favour showing to which Clan the wearer belonged. The laws were enforced with rigorous brutality, and were not rescinded until 1782, by which time the last vestiges of the old fighting Clans had disappeared.

It was also the end of the direct line of descendants as Chiefs of the Clan Maclean. Sir Hector had never married and left no heir. His third cousin Allan Maclean of Brolass was the nearest surviving kin and the baronetcy devolved on him. But it wasn't a complete break with the direct line because Allan Maclean was descended directly from Hector Og, 15th Chief through his second marriage.

Sir Allan Maclean was the sixth baronet of Morvern, and like his predecessors and those who were to follow him as Chief of the Clan, his life was to be spent in military service. His early career in the Army was spent abroad fighting for Holland; then he was commissioned into the Montgomery Highlanders and as Captain General of nine companies fought in America until the final conquest of Canada in 1760. When he finally left the Army it was with the rank of colonel and with the pension which was his only income he leased the tiny island of Inchkenneth off the coast of Mull. It was the nearest Sir Allan could get to Duart, still the spiritual home of all Macleans. Before Sir Allan and his three daughters moved to Inchkenneth, the island had been uninhabited and during his lifetime the family remained as its only residents – Lady Maclean had died while her husband was serving in America. The pension he received from the Army must have been a generous one because he apparently lived in some style at Inchkenneth and also involved himself in a costly and lengthy law suit against the fifth Duke of Argyll. The dispute was over the ownership of Maclean lands at Brolass. The Argyll family had already driven the Macleans from Duart and the castle had been deliberately vandalised and left roofless and ruined to become derelict for the next 150 years. But they also claimed the rights of Brolass under a contract signed by Sir Lachlan Maclean in 1634.

Sir Allan carried on the legal battle for nearly twenty years and it was only in the year he died, 1783, that the matter was finally resolved in a partial victory which gave back to the Maclean family some of their lands.

As Sir Allan Maclean, who died in 1783, was survived by only female children, his titles passed to yet another branch of the family. This time to a cousin, Hector Maclean also a descendant of Hector Og of Brolass.

Sir Hector Maclean became 23rd Chief and seventh Baronet of Morvern and was Chief from 1783 until his death in 1818. He too was an officer in the Army for a time but there is little record of any distinction in his career and he appears to have spent the major part of his life living in quiet seclusion. He was married, but his wife failed to produce any children and on his death the titles passed to his half-brother Sir Fitzroy Jeffreys Grafton Maclean as 24th Chief of the Clan Maclean. Sir Fitzroy was born to Sir Allan Maclean's second wife Margaret, whose Irish ancestry was reflected in the names she gave her son, Jeffreys Grafton, names which had no connection with the Maclean family until that time.

But the new Chief inherited the Maclean love of soldiering and became one of the most successful of his Clan, rising to the rank of General in his fifty years in the Army.

He spent twenty-eight of those years serving in the West Indies, where he was made Governor General of the Islands of St Thomas and St John from 1808 to 1815. When he returned to Britain he made his home in London, continuing the tradition of Maclean Chiefs who were to live outside Scotland. He was married twice, the first time to the widow of John Bishop of Barbados, by whom he had two surviving sons, Charles Fitzroy and Donald, and then on the death of his wife he remarried, again to a widow, from Sussex this time, by whom there were no children.

Both sons had successful careers, the younger Donald became a Member of Parliament, and married a general's daughter with whom he lived happily, until he died in 1874; while the elder son Charles Fitzroy was to follow his father into the Army where he started a new Maclean tradition by joining the Scots Guards.

Sir Charles Fitzroy Maclean became 25th Chief of the Clan in 1847 on the death of his father. He was the first Chief for many generations who took a more than passing interest in the history of the Clan and it was he who was responsible for instilling in his sons and heir the urge to regain and restore Duart Castle. Sir Charles became an expert in the affairs of the Macleans and an authority on Highland customs and dress. When an attempt was made to abolish the wearing of Highland dress in the Army, Sir Charles took a leading role in opposing the change and was successful in preventing such a controversial and unfair regulation from being introduced.

In 1831, Sir Fitzroy married Emily Eleanor, daughter of the Rev Jacob Marsham, Dean of Windsor by whom he had five children, one son and four daughters. His son Fitzroy was to become the outstanding Chief of modern times and one of the most romantic figures in recent Scottish history, while his daughters are all worthy of mention. The first, Emily was to provide her brother with the money with which he was able to buy back the ruins of Duart Castle and begin the massive programme of restoration work; Lousia married the second son of the Earl of Abergavenny; Fanny married the distinguished sailor Sir A W A Hood (later 1st Baron Hood of Avalon) of the Royal Navy, and Marcia, the baby of the family, became the wife of Charles Rolls (1st Baron Llangatock) whose collaboration with Sir Henry Royce was to result in the world's finest motor car.

Sir Charles and his family lived abroad for much of the time; in Ireland, where Fitzroy was born in Dublin; in Gibraltar and Malta, and in England, where they had homes in London and on the Kent coast in Folkestone.

They spent very little time in Scotland, usually only when they sailed around the Western Isles. On these occasions Sir Charles would remain on board and members of the Clan would visit him to pay homage to their Chief. It is said that he never once set foot on Mull itself, refusing to land while Duart was not in the possession of the Macleans. He allowed his children to visit Duart, but preferred to watch from the sea as they scampered about the ruined battlements of their ancestral home.

Sir Charles spent the summer months at his home in Folkestone on the Kent coast and in the latter years of his life he began to spend even more time there. It was at West Cliffe House in Folkestone that he died in December, 1883.

His heir and the new Chief of the Clan Maclean was Sir Fitzroy Donald Maclean, 10th Baronet and 26th Chief. This was the man who, though born in Ireland and who lived for most of his lifetime away from Scotland, came to be recognised as a 'true Highlander' and someone for whom the cause of the Macleans became a sacred crusade. Fitzroy Maclean was born on 18th May, 1835 in Dublin where his father was Commanding Officer of the 81st Regiment. When he was a few weeks old he was taken from Ireland to Yorkshire where his grandfather the Reverend the Hon John Marsham, who was also Canon of Windsor, had another living at Kirkby, Overblow. Within three years, the family suffered a major tragedy when Fitzroy's mother died in childbirth at Gibraltar where Sir Charles's regiment was then stationed. She and her infant son were buried at Gibraltar and the immediate responsibility for bringing up the remaining five children fell to her sister, Miss Marianne Marsham, who willingly carried out these duties, and continued to act as surrogate mother until her death in 1889.

In the meantime Sir Charles, who had inherited the baronetcy in 1847, was posted to Malta, and his family joined him for much of the time, living on the Mediterranean island and cruising in his yacht to most of the major ports of Italy and Sicily. The family returned to England in 1849 and young Fitzroy was educated privately at home, which was then in Cockenhall in Durham. He was also sent to Germany for a time to study the language.

The Macleans lived very comfortably with Sir Charles spending a great deal of his time sailing his yacht around the coast of Britain and across the North Sea to Scandinavia, but always making sure that they were at Cowes during the week of the Royal Regatta. When Sir Charles went to Dublin he took young Fitzroy with him and called on His Royal Highness, the Duke of Connaught, son of Queen Victoria, who was an old friend. The Duke in turn visited the Macleans on board their yacht and then invited them to spend a day with him at Phoenix Park.

It was a foregone conclusion that Fitzroy would follow his father into the Army via Sandhurst and in preparation for the entrance examination he was sent to Paris to study French, as modern languages were to be his speciality. In the 19th century officers were required to be confirmed into the Church of England and so before Fitzroy was allowed into Sandhurst he was confirmed by the Bishop of Durham. The importance of the Maclean family in the area at the time can be gauged by the fact that he was the only candidate for confirmation and a special service was held at Bishop Auckland to enable him to fulfill his entrance requirements. In those days commissions in the Army had to be bought, and Fitzroy's father paid £800 for his son to become a Cornet in the 7th Dragoon Guards. Pay for a Cornet was eight shillings a day, from which a half a crown (12½p) was deducted for the upkeep of his horse. Sir Charles Maclean received a letter advising him that his son had been commissioned on the 17th August, 1852. It reads:

Lieutenant General Lord Fitzroy Somerset [later Lord Raglan] presents his compliments to Sir C Fitzroy Maclean and has the honour to acquaint him by direction of the Commander in Chief, that Her Majesty has been pleased to appoint Mr Fitzroy Donald Maclean to a Cornetcy by purchase in the 7th Dragoon Guards.

The Commission itself was signed by the Duke of Wellington.

When he took up his first appointment in the Dragoon Guards he was personally welcomed to St James's Palace by no less a person than Prince Albert, Queen Victoria's Consort. In 1854 to 1855 he served in Bulgaria and the Crimea, during which time he avidly kept a diary of the day-to-day events. Names from the annals of military history such as Lord Raglan, Lord Cardigan and Lord Harlech occur frequently and one excerpt from a single day's entry reveals the extent of discipline that characterised the Army of that time:

Sunday, 23rd July 1854, Varna, Turkey – Church Parade. Did not feel well, it was a very hot morning, but resumed my duties later on as Orderly Officer. Two Turkish soldiers found horse stealing in the Infantry Camp. Taken before the Provost Sergeant of the 88th and both flogged.

And the rigours of the campaign are underlined in this excerpt relating to one of the many deaths from cholera which attacked all ranks, common soldiers and officers alike:

. . . We have just heard that one of our corporals has died from Cholera . . . when a man dies he is just sewn up in his cloak and left in front of the Guard Tent . . . this is how a poor fellow ends his days in Bulgaria . . .

He fought at the Battle of Alma and witnessed scenes which he afterwards claimed could never be effaced from his memory, and he missed the Charge of the Light Brigade only because he happened to be on sick report on that fateful day. While in hospital at Scutari, he met Florence Nightingale, but reported that 'she only nursed the men, not the officers.'

He was decorated for gallantry in the Crimea and survived hand-fighting, disease, hunger and extremes of weather before being sent back to England at the end of the war.

Sir Fitzroy continued his overseas travels throughout his life. In Rome he was received in audience by Pope Pius IX and stayed with his uncle Donald Maclean at the villa near Naples which was subsequently to become his through a legacy. His military career reads like a 'boys own' paper story: service in Ireland where he regularly lunched with the

Prince of Wales; tea parties attended by Queen Victoria where he recalled that ' . . . I once had the honour of handing Her Majesty a cup of tea . . . '; manouvers in France where he became a companion of the Emperor Napoleon III and three years in Canada and the United States of America, where he met and became friends with Jefferson David, the former President of the Confederate States (after his release from prison).

It was when his regiment returned from Canada that Fitzroy met the woman who was to be become his wife at a dinner party given by his sister (later Lady Llangattock). By a series of coincidences Fitzroy and Constance Ackers were to meet a number of times both in England and Ireland during the next few months, and no one was surprised when they announced their engagement. They were married in 1872 at St James's Church Piccadilly and the only thing to mar their happiness was when the bride's father died just three days after the wedding.

A year later, on 17th February, 1873, their first son Hector Charles was born at Aldershot. The same year Sir Fitzroy decided to leave the Army after twenty-one years' service for family reasons. On his final day he presented his charger to Queen Victoria, who provided the mare with a comfortable home for the rest of her days in the mews at Buckingham Palace and later at Hampton Court. After the mare died, her hooves were sent to Sir Fitzroy who had them made as a base for a silver candelabra which can be seen today in the Banqueting Hall at Duart Castle.

Another son, Charles Lachlan was born in 1874, on the 20th September, the anniversary of the Battle of Alma.

During his twenty-one years in the Army, Fitzroy Maclean had risen from the most junior rank of Cornet to the Command of his regiment as Lieutenant-Colonel. He had taken part in some of the most historic battles of the century, met many of the world's leading figures and ridden in the funeral procession of the Duke of Wellington. But that wasn't the end of his military career. Three years after retiring from the Army as a full-time officer he became involved in reforming the West Kent Yeomanry, and went on to command the regiment for more than nineteen years.

Two more sons were born: Fitzroy Holland in 1876, who died at the age of five in 1881, and John Marsham in 1879. His only daughter Finovola was the last of his children, born on 14th February, 1887, four years after Fitzroy had succeeded to the baronetcy on the death of his father in 1883. He was the 26th Chief of the Clan Maclean and it was around this time, the latter part of the 19th century, that he began to have serious thoughts about regaining Duart for the Maclean Clan.

The castle had changed hands several times since the Argyll family had gained control after the 1745 rebellion and for some years it had been part of the estate owned by the Guthrie family. Sir Fitzroy made a number of visits to Mull where he was received kindly by the Guthries.

Sir Fitzroy realised the feeling of the Macleans for their Clan and for their Chief, particularly on a visit to America when he was introduced to hundreds to Macleans in a dozen cities, all of whom were delighted to recognise him as their Chief.

In 1892 the first Clan Gathering was held in Glasgow with some 200 clansfolk attending and this became an annual event interrupted only by the war years. The Clan Maclean Association has grown with the century so that today it has more than 2,000 members in almost every country in the world. The President of the Association is Sir Fitzroy Maclean Bt, one of the most distinguished soldiers of the Second World War, a former member of Parliament and a noteworthy author with a number of bestselling books to his credit. Fitzroy Maclean is a Chieftain of Clan Maclean, styled as Maclean of Dunconner, with his own sept based at Strachur on the banks of Loch Fine where he is host to celebrities from all over the world who come to stay at his charming hotel.

The headquarters of the Clan Maclean Association is located in a tenement house in Glasgow where Mrs Detta Maclean has acted as secretary for nearly twenty years. Detta Maclean lives and breathes Clan Maclean. She is in close contact with branches in Australia and the USA and tells tales of being woken in the middle of the night by parties of Macleans who have travelled thousands of miles to Scotland and are *en route* to Duart. 'I'm always glad to see them', she says, 'but I wish sometimes they would adjust their personal clocks from Australian to British time.'

Members of the association are put in touch with each other and discuss such matters as geneology, tartans (which is the correct way for a lady to wear a sash?), how to cook a haggis, Highland customs, Clan marches and poems and in particular any stories of Maclean history which can be added to the fund of knowledge already stored in the Clan records. The Clan has a large collection of books, manuscrips and papers relating to the Macleans which is now lodged in the Mitchell Library, Glasgow. Members of the association and serious students of the Highland Clan system are allowed access to the collection, but nothing is permitted to leave the premises.

Detta Maclean claims that every significant Maclean in the world is a member of the Association, including such disparate talents as Alistair Maclean, one of the biggest selling authors in the world, and Tom Maclean, who in 1982 rowed across the Atlantic singlehanded in the smallest boat ever to complete the crossing. There is even a Clan historian, The Rev. Allan Maclean.

Old Sir Fitzroy continued in public life after he retired from the Army. He was a Justice of the Peace in Kent where he spent part of his year in the family home at Folkestone he had inherited, and in 1900 he was elected President of the Highland Society of London. In 1904 he was made a Knight Commander of the Order of the Bath by King Edward VII, and in 1907 he was invited to become President of the League of Mercy.

His youngest son, John Marsham, who was commissioned in the Royal Field Artillery, served in the South African War and was killed in action on 3rd November, 1901.

In 1911 after several years of friendly negotiations, not over the price, but because the family of Mr. Guthrie who owned Duart did not wish to sell in his lifetime, the castle became the property of Sir Fitzroy Maclean on the instructions of Mrs. Guthrie. He wrote in his diary that on the day it became his, he felt at last 'Maclean has come into his own again.'

The restoration of Duart Castle has been written about in a separate chapter. Suffice it to say that it was the dream of a lifetime come true and there were just three more significant dates to be recorded in the story of Fitzroy Maclean.

In 1912 the first Clan Gathering was held at Duart Castle when the Maclean banner was raised. In 1935 there was a further celebration on the occasion of the Chief's one hundredth birthday and then finally and sadly, in 1936 at the age of 101, old Sir Fitzroy died. He was the longest lived of any of the Chiefs and in many ways he had achieved more than any of his predecessors. His eldest son and rightful heir had died before him and so the mantle of Chiefship was to fall on the youthful shoulders of his grandson Chips. Sir Charles Hector Fitzroy Maclean – 27th Chief of the Clan Maclean.

CONCLUSION

When Chips retired as Lord Chamberlain in December, 1984 he was able to look back with a certain amount of satisfaction on a job well done. He had entered Royal service with no previous experience of Court life and he had stage-managed some of the most important and spectacular events in modern history.

When he first went to St James's Palace it was without any real knowledge of what the job entailed and yet by the time he left, he was considered one of the outstanding Lord Chamberlain's of this century.

Chips and Elizabeth had become an integral part of the Royal Household and if she was regarded as the outgoing and ever cheerful extrovert, who revelled in the diplomatic round of parties and other functions, he was equally at home in Royal circles and has been described by his friends as the 'consummate courtier'. Between running the Royal Household and his many other duties, he was responsible for arranging the funerals of the Duke of Gloucester and the Duke of Windsor (probably the most difficult royal occasion since the Abdication) and the weddings of Princess Anne and later the Prince of Wales.

Throughout his thirteen years as Head of the Queen's Household, he was required to maintain a delicate balance between being a showman and a diplomat. He was all too aware of the need to allow public access to the great Royal occasions via the press and the television cameras, at the same time making sure that the dignity of the events was sustained. Hence his surprise at the display of balloons tied to the carriage of the Prince and Princess of Wales as they left Buckingham Palace on honeymoon.

His attention to detail became a byword in palace circles and his unending courtesy was known to everyone who came in contact with him, from the most junior employee of Her Majesty to the Heads of State of the most powerful countries in the world. When he was offered the position of Lord Chamberlain he talked it over with Elizabeth, who for the first and only time in her life gave him an ultimatum. She said, 'I hope this is a job for both of us because I am not going to remain at Duart on my own.' And Chips is the first to acknowledge that if he has achieved any success as Lord Chamberlain it is greatly due to the support that his wife has given him so unstintingly. While his own unique talents have carried him gracefully through some of the most ticklish problems of Royal protocol, it was Elizabeth who made their apartment in St James's Palace into the warm, welcoming home from home for so many visitors from overseas. Her friendliness extended to all and sundry. Their neighbours included Princess Alexandra described by many as 'the nicest of all the Royal Family', and Elizabeth remembers young Lord Nicholas Windsor roller-skating around Friary Court, and then hinting very strongly that an ice cream would be most welcome, to which she replied: 'Come on in then, but take your skates off first, I'm not having them on my dining-room carpet.'

For both Chips and Elizabeth it was a very special time in their lives. They thoroughly enjoyed living in St James's Palace and, as they both said later, 'attending some of the most marvellous occasions we would not otherwise have had the privilege of attending.' Elizabeth regarded her role as Lord Chamberlain's wife as being one where her aim was to make all the other wives feel at home, particularly those from abroad who perhaps felt a little out of their depth in the sophisticated surroundings of the Royal Palaces. Summing up, Elizabeth said:

It really was the most marvellous period. We met so many interesting people, the Prime Ministers of the day, some of whom have remained good friends. We were blessed with living in that beautiful house and of course privileged in working for such a wonderful family for such a long time.

When they left St James's Palace the break was absolute. Neither Chips nor Elizabeth wanted to keep going back and it's a fact that when a member of the Royal Household leaves he is not usually encouraged to start visiting his old office too frequently. The old adage 'The King is Dead, Long Live the King' applies not only to the sovereign.

For Chips though, the break was not to be absolutely final. The Queen decided to appoint him Chief Steward at Hampton Court Palace. The Palace has not been lived in by Royalty since the early part of the 18th century and much of it is used these days as Grace-and-Favour homes. In addition Chips has been appointed a permanent Lord-in-Waiting to the Queen so he remains on the strength of the Household.

He is also still Lord Lieutenant of the County of Argyll, a position he has held for more than thirty years and one in which he takes a great deal of pride. As with most of the other appointments which have come his way, the Lord Lieutenancy of Argyll came to him out of the blue and as a complete surprise. He first heard the rumour while attending the funeral service for the late Bruce Campbell, the previous holder of the office. The Campbell family had been Lords Lieutenant of

Argyll for generations and when someone whispered in Chips' ear that he was to be the next Lord Lieutenant he thought the man was mad. Although this particular branch of the Campbells had been friends of the Macleans for many years, there was still a certain amount of wary rivalry between the two main families and the break with tradition must have come as a bit of a shock. But there was a delightfully pleasant sequel to Chips' appointment. On the day he was made Lord Lieutenant of the County, he received from Bruce Campbell's son, the Lord Lieutenant's flag which his father had flown on his car. It was the kindest gesture of reconciliation and one which was greatly appreciated by Chips.

To the rest of the Clan Maclean the appointment of their Chief as Lord Lieutenant was a matter of enormous pride. Sir Fitzroy Maclean believes it was one of the most significant Scottish appointments of the early postwar years and he says it was probably through knowing Chips as Lord Lieutenant initially that the Queen eventually made him her Lord Chamberlain. Because this was the beginning of the relationship between Chips Maclean and the Royal Family. In August 1958, the Queen, the Duke of Edinburgh, the Prince of Wales and Princess Anne spent two hours having tea at Duart, and being shown around the castle after landing from *Britannia*, while on their annual cruise of the Western Isles, and some time later, Prince Philip, who was sailing along the west coast of Scotland in his yawl *Bloodhound*, took shelter in Duart Bay when storms broke out. Sir Charles (as he then was) and Lady Maclean were delighted to welcome the Royal party ashore for a drink before they continued their cruise the next morning.

At this time Chips was living permanently at Duart, and he decided that as the land was not suitable for arable farming he would try his hand at raising a pedigree herd of Highland cattle. At first he was reasonably successful and the quality of his animals bore comparison with any in the country, but there were a number of factors against his herd becoming a long-term success. First there was the lack of space. His land was too small to sustain a herd large enough for it to be economic, and as his own knowledge of the business was obviously limited, he had to employ someone else to look after them, thereby adding to the costs.

Looking back Chips realises that realistically he was on a non-starter from the beginning as far as running the herd as a profitable business venture, and all it became was a very expensive hobby. By the time he had got out of breeding Highland cattle, he had lost money – and learned a lot. 'It was a very interesting experience', he says, 'but it was never going to make a profit, so I had to sell.'

In 1965 he was invited to join the Royal Company of Archers as a

Brigadier (now a Lieutenant). The Queen's Bodyguard for Scotland is one of the most exclusive organisations in the land and to serve in its ranks is a signal honour. One of his fellow Archers is Lord Cathcart, who had served with him in the Scots Guards, and who had gone on to command the regiment. However in the hierarchy of the Royal Company of Archers the colonel was junior to the major.

Public appointments and further honours were beginning to come his way with what many of his fellow Scots regard as the ultimate accolade arriving in 1968 when he was made a Knight of the Thistle.

Lord Home of the Hirsel and Sir Fitzroy Maclean are both in no doubt whatever that for Chips to be created a Knight of the Thistle was the highest honour that can be awarded to any Scotsman. Chips remembers the day he learned that he was being offered the opportunity of joining the Most Noble Order. 'I was at home in Duart when the telephone rang and it was Martin Charteris, the Queen's Assistant Private Secretary who simply said, "The Queen would like you to become a Knight of the Thistle." It was as bald as that.' It came as a complete surprise, just like most of his other appointments, but one which gave, and still gives him a deep sense of pride and honour. He says, 'I know that the Thistle is regarded as the pinnacle of achievement for a Scot. I regard it even more so for a Highlander, which is what I am.'

What it really means was finally brought home to him one day not long after he had been installed as a Knight of the Thistle. He was in St Giles Cathedral in Edinburgh when he heard someone taking a party of visitors around the cathedral. As they paused near the Chapel of the Order of the Thistle, the guide pointed out the various ancient banners and just as Chips was passing by he heard the guide say 'and that's the Maclean standard.' 'It was the moment,' he says, 'that I realised what it meant to be included in the history of the Order of the Thistle.' So he joined the rest of the tour to see if he could find out any more about himself.

In his so-called retirement Chips divides his time between Wilderness House – where he is so busy with his private correspondence that he has to employ a part-time secretary – the House of Lords, Duart Castle and the Distiller's Company of which he is a non-executive director. He also found time to write a children's book (before he retired) and perhaps he will continue as a literary laird when time allows.

The problem of what to do with Duart occupies much of his attention and that of his son and heir Lachlan. It's a millstone which can never be run at a profit and the financial problems are frightening to consider. He says, 'Every time it rains it seems like it's another thousand pounds'. But on one thing he and Lachlan are determined and that is that Duart must be saved at all costs. How this is to be achieved has not been decided. Lachlan is more pragmatic than his father and he feels that perhaps it might be better to turn the castle into a charitable trust, linked to the Maclean Clan. Chips is not sure what the solution is. He and Lachlan have recently had discussions with their architect to find out the true extent of what needs to be done to preserve the castle. 'Duart was out of the family for two centuries and that's far too long,' says Chips, who determined that whatever happens (or almost), the castle will survive. There's only one condition he imposes on his heirs regarding the future of Duart: 'I would rather see it crumble to nothing than it should fall into the hands of the Campbells once more'.

He has been head of the Clan for fifty years, which makes him one of the longest-serving Chiefs in Scotland. He was Lord High Commissioner of the Church of Scotland on two occasions, Chief Commissioner of Scouts for Scotland for five years and Chief Scout of the United Kingdom and the Commonwealth for thirteen years. He was a member of a brave and exclusive regiment for more than ten years and reached the highest position in the Queen's service as Lord Chamberlain.

As he looks back on a career that had been distinguished in so many areas what for him would be his ideal epitaph? He has no hesitation in choosing what he would like to be remembered for. Like his grandfather before him and all the Macleans stretching back to the 12th century, there is only one description he truly cares for: 'He is a Highlander.'

APPENDIX

Chiefs of the Clan Maclean

1. Gillean of the Battleaxe
2. Gille-Iosa
3. Malcolm
4. Ian Dubh – Black John
5. Lachlan Lubanach
6. Eachann Ruadh nan Cath – Red Hector
7. Lachlan Bronnach
8. Lachlan Og
9. Hector the Swarthy
10. Lachlan
11. Lachlan Catanach
12. Hector Mor
13. Hector Og
14. Lachlan Mor Maclean
15. Eachann Og
16. Eachann Mor
17. Sir Lachlan Maclean, Bt.
18. Sir Eachann Ruadh
19. Sir Allen Maclean, Bt.
20. Sir John Maclean, Bt.
21. Sir Hector Maclean, Bt.
22. Sir Allan Maclean, Bt.
23. Sir Hector Maclean, Bt.
24. Sir Fitzroy Jeffreys Grafton Maclean, Bt.
25. Sir Charles Fitzroy Maclean, Bt.
26. Sir Fitzroy Donald Maclean, Bt.
27. Maclean of Duart

INDEX